I have enjoyed competing against and working with a guy [Mike Singletary] who is so consistent in his walk.

Ozzie Newsome
GENERAL MANAGER AND EXECUTIVE VICE PRESIDENT
BALTIMORE RAVENS;
NFL HALL OF FAMER

Before we can sell anyone on the integrity of God's Word, we have to sell them on the integrity of *our* word. Mike Singletary has done this by how he played football, how he has lived his life off the field and how he now leads others. When you have finished reading this book, you will know what makes Mike a man with character and integrity, and you will have gained new insights into how to become the person of integrity that you want to be.

John C. Maxwell
BEST-SELLING AUTHOR AND SPEAKER

More important than having been one of the greatest football players of our time, Mike Singletary is a man of high integrity, whose character is an example to all.

Mike Nolan
HEAD COACH OF THE SAN FRANCISCO 49ERS

The Fellowship of Christian Athletes has been blessed to have Mike Singletary as a Christian ambassador to the world of sports. He is the ultimate servant-leader, on and off the field of competition. As an NFL coach and as a Hall of Fame linebacker, he truly models Jesus, mentors others and manages his life according to God's principles. His passion and intensity for the game of football is only surpassed by his love for Jesus and his family. His spiritual insights will inspire and impact your life profoundly.

Les Steckel
PRESIDENT
FELLOWSHIP OF CHRISTIAN ATHLETES

Mike Singletary One-on-One is an inspirational combination of Mike's life experiences and the wisdom of the Bible. We can all learn from the life lessons in this book. Mike is a real guy who truly walks his talk.

Matt Stover
KICKER, BALTIMORE RAVENS

In addition to teaching techniques and the fundamentals of the game, coaches and teachers should strive to be the kind of example that students look up to and desire to emulate. Mike Singletary has modeled a strategy that can be used both on and off the field. His new book, *Mike Singletary One on One,* is not only inspirational but also instructional to the point that the contents can be used as a game plan for one's life. Coauthor Jay Carty unfolds the biblical principles that will apply to everyday challenges. As you read Mike's book of 60 stories from his life, listen to what is being taught, ask yourself questions and then take Mike's advice.

Grant Teaff
EXECUTIVE DIRECTOR, AMERICAN FOOTBALL COACHES ASSOCIATION
HEAD FOOTBALL COACH, BAYLOR UNIVERSITY (1972-1992)

Ability may get you to the top, but it takes character to keep you there. As a player, a coach and a man of faith, Mike has proven that he has both ability and character. He is a solid addition to the One-on-One series.

John Wooden
UCLA BASKETBALL HEAD COACH (1948-1975)
BASKETBALL HALL OF FAME
COAUTHOR, *COACH WOODEN'S PYRAMID OF SUCCESS* AND *COACH WOODEN ONE-ON-ONE*

MIKE SINGLETARY

SINGLETARY

ONE-ON-ONE

MIKE SINGLETARY

JAY CARTY

Regal

From Gospel Light
Ventura, California, U.S.A.

PUBLISHED BY REGAL BOOKS
FROM GOSPEL LIGHT
VENTURA, CALIFORNIA, U.S.A.
PRINTED IN THE U.S.A.

Regal Books is a ministry of Gospel Light, a Christian publisher dedicated to serving the local church. We believe God's vision for Gospel Light is to provide church leaders with biblical, user-friendly materials that will help them evangelize, disciple and minister to children, youth and families.

It is our prayer that this Regal book will help you discover biblical truth for your own life and help you meet the needs of others. May God richly bless you.

For a free catalog of resources from Regal Books/Gospel Light, please call your Christian supplier or contact us at 1-800-4-GOSPEL *or* www.regalbooks.com.

Library of Congress Cataloging-in-Publication Data

Singletary, Mike.
   Mike Singletary one-on-one / Mike Singletary, Jay Carty.
      p. cm.
   Includes bibliographical references.
   ISBN 0-8307-3702-2 (hard cover)
   1. Christian life—Meditations.   I. Carty, Jay. II. Title.
BV4501.3.S577 2005
242—dc22   2005015388

1 2 3 4 5 6 7 8 9 10 11 12 13 14 15 / 11 10 09 08 07 06 05

Rights for publishing this book in other languages are contracted by Gospel Light Worldwide, the international nonprofit ministry of Gospel Light. Gospel Light Worldwide also provides publishing and technical assistance to international publishers dedicated to producing Sunday School and Vacation Bible School curricula and books in the languages of the world. For additional information, visit www.gospellightworldwide.org; write to Gospel Light Worldwide, P.O. Box 3875, Ventura, CA 93006; or send an e-mail to info@gospellightworldwide.org.

DEDICATION

From Mike Singletary

to every man and woman who has been given the awesome responsibility of coaching, at any level. You have been entrusted with the hearts, minds and souls of these young men and women. May you purpose in your heart to develop in them character first, skill and talent second. You have incredible input into their lives. Use it to bring forth goodness and honor.

From Jay Carty
to

the Turners, Knechts and Eneys.
You are dear friends whom the Lord sent at just the right time.

CONTENTS

ACKNOWLEDGMENTS

Thanks from
Mike Singletary
to

my mother, Rudell, for her devotion to raising me in the fear and admonition of the Lord. I know she was greeted in heaven with the words "Well done, my good and faithful servant."

my dad, for deciding it's never too late to restore a relationship. I have enjoyed these last 20 years. I love you.

my brothers and sisters. We've got to continue to grow closer as our numbers dwindle.

my in-laws. I couldn't ask for better. You have supported and encouraged us and set an example of a faithful family.

Gerald Watson. I am humbled by your obedience to continuously pray for me. I know that the path God has me on is a direct result of the time you have spent on your knees on my behalf.

and to Kim. You are my best friend, a wonderful wife and an outstanding mother to our kids. You are loved and cherished by all who know you. In short, you are the answer to my prayers.

Thanks from
Jay Carty
to
Sam Talbert

You did it again, Sam. Thanks.

INTRODUCTION

HIS EYES

BY JAY CARTY

Roll a highlights video of classic moments in the NFL and we will see:

- Dick Butkus snarling, covered in mud and blood, tape hanging from his wrist.
- Bart Starr plunging into the end zone for a quarterback sneak on the frozen tundra of Lambeau Field.
- The 49ers' Dwight Clark coming out of nowhere to grab "The Catch" from Joe Montana.
- Mike Singletary's stare.

Mona Lisa had her smile. Mike has his eyes. Peering out from his helmet, his gaze pierced like a laser beam. The intensity showed, but number 50's eyes on television and on the cover of *Sports Illustrated* didn't do him justice. I first saw Mike's eyes in real life when I met the NFL Hall-of-Fame linebacker at a Pro Athletes Outreach conference. The shake of his hand was warm, genial. His look was solid, intense. At the conference his eyes conveyed an extreme passion for Jesus, but I found myself wondering what it would have been like as an opposing lineman with those same eyes and that same passion directed toward me. No wonder he made the Pro Bowl 10 times and is listed as one of the top 100 football players of all time.

Mike Singletary played his college ball at Baylor University where he averaged more than 15 tackles a game. Three times he had more than 30 tackles in a single game and in the 1978 season he made 232 tackles. He was twice named an All-American. Mike hit opposing players so hard that he split 16 helmets during his college years.

Mike Singletary was a second-round selection by the Chicago Bears in the 1981 NFL draft. Most teams that had considered drafting Mike wanted him to play fullback, believing he was too small to play linebacker. However, Mike insisted on staying in his chosen position, even if it meant going lower in the draft. By his seventh game in a Bear uniform, he was the starting middle linebacker, a position he played for 12 seasons. Ten times he was named to the Pro Bowl team and twice he was the NFL's defensive player of the year. His numbers are impressive: 172 starts, 1488 tackles, 19 sacks and 7 interceptions. He is arguably the most complete linebacker ever to play the game. He hit harder than any of his peers and covered receivers as well as anybody in the game ever has. No linebacker before or since has done both so well.

In 1985, Mike led the Chicago defense that only allowed opponents to score 11 points per game and sparked Coach Mike Ditka's Bears to a 15-1 record. Chicago won the Super Bowl that season.

Mike Singletary only missed two games during his NFL career. After the 1991 season, he called it quits as a player. By then, his place as one of the all-time greats was secure. Mike no longer played middle linebacker, but he did not lose his intensity and dedication—he just applied it in other areas and grew as a person. He polished his communication skills and hit the road on the speaking circuit, both in churches and in the corporate world. He launched the Leadership Zone and marketed his leadership concepts. And he dedicated himself to his family and church.

Mike waited a decade before taking his first shot at coaching. He started as linebacker coach with the Ravens in 2003. Two years later—in 2005—he accepted the position of assistant head coach and linebacker coach with the San Francisco 49ers.

Mike Singletary is committed to working with 49ers head coach Mike Nolan to restore the 49ers as a winning team. Mike also has aspirations of being an NFL head coach himself; but for now, he sees himself as being in a season of preparation.

When Mike Singletary and I sat down to work on this book, he lived in the suburbs of Baltimore, a ten-minute drive from the Ravens' practice facility. (Mike and his family have since moved to the Bay Area.) Mike and his wife, Kim, were gracious hosts. All seven of the Singletary children were amazingly polite, not only to me, but also to our servers at our meal together in a restaurant. They were also fun and loving, and kind to each other as well as to others. I could see that they enjoyed each other immensely. It was wonderful to see everyone participate in the family fun, including the six-year-old.

Kim is amazing as a mother to her children and as a wife to Mike. She ably juggles meals, games, school functions and lessons of all sorts. She is an exceptional woman: thoughtful, funny and full of grace.

The night I arrived in Baltimore, Mike was at a preseason game, so Kim was there to pick me up. I had gone east to spend time with Mike working on this book. The three of us arrived at the Singletary's home at about the same time. I was surprised at how easily Mike shifted from one hot seat to another. He went from giving instructions as a coach to recounting myriad details of his life and career without missing a beat—moreover, he never lost his passion. Even when Mike Singletary relaxes, he does so with intensity.

He is the most intense man I have ever met.

Mike is intentional about everything he does. There were no wasted moments. We fit our work in where we could. We even talked in the car on the freeway while going to his son's football game, during breaks between coaches' meetings, at lunch time and after his family time, late into the evening. He never wasted a moment during that visit nor during our subsequent discussions in preparing this manuscript. I think as you read you will feel a bit of his intensity, too.

Mike has his workout equipment in his home. He has always done his off-season and preseason weight training alone. That gives us another clue as to his disciplined nature. It's not easy to push yourself without help. But he did it for 12 years as a Bear. These days, Mike weighs in at 218 and measures only 4 percent body fat. Not bad! On the practice field I watched him jog over to his coaching station. He still runs like an athlete, and his eyes haven't changed.

Mike is single-minded about seeking and doing God's will. His focus is on his prime directive of being the best possible Christian, husband, father and coach he can be—in that order. He is in love with Jesus Christ and totally committed to obeying God's Word. As a husband Mike is lovingly thoughtful; as a dad he is a firm disciplinarian but tender in the process. As a coach, he is like a pastor caring for his flock.

This is the third One-on-One book I have cowritten. I had the honor of teaming up with legendary coach John Wooden and NASCAR great Darrell Waltrip on the first two. As in the other One-on-One books, *Mike Singletary One-On-One* is intended to be read as a devotional. And we want you to interact. On the first page of each reading, Mike recounts a story from his life—many of these stories read like an NFL highlight film! On the next page, I take you further into the point of the day. Sometimes I draw from my experiences, other times I simply plug you into a biblical perspective. At the end of each reading, we include a prayer and suggested Bible verses to study.

As you read each entry, imagine number 50's eyes peering at you from inside his helmet. Picture the NFL Hall of Famer passionately prodding you to be more like Jesus. Then, as you say the prayer and read the verses, imagine Jesus' eyes gazing at you with grace, hope and promise.

Tighten up your chinstrap. We're going one-on-one.

AN OFF-ROAD LIFE

BY KIM SINGLETARY

My oldest daughter, Kristen, has just graduated from high school. Like every 18-year-old, she faces choices about her future, specifically which college to attend. Applying, waiting, wondering, anticipating with Kristen takes me back.

Deciding where one will spend his or her college years is huge. There are so many questions to ask: How far should I be away from my family? How large should the school be? What should my major be? Which program has the most respect in the business world? Which school has the best-possible mates? I must confess that I wish I had put a little more thought into this life-altering decision than I did when I went off to college.

For Mike, it was much different than for me. He was highly sought after by Baylor University's football coach, Grant Teaff. I was a young coed coming to Waco, Texas, from the North. Little did I know that the whole civil war thing hadn't really been laid to rest!

In 1978, I was a senior in high school in Sterling Heights, Michigan, a suburb of Detroit. My family was no different from most in our neighborhood. My father worked at General Motors and my mother stayed home until the college tuition bills came in—mine were the first for our family. I had fairly good grades and knew I wanted to go to college; I just didn't know where. We were Baptists and my parents wanted me to go to a Christian school, but none in the area were particularly appealing to me. My dad worked with a gentleman whose daughter attended Baylor. He said, "All I know is she never wants to come home during the breaks."

The thought of warmer winters was attractive to me. Moreover, Baylor had a swim team (I swam competitively for my high school) and a great law school (at the time I had delusions of grandeur). I knew Baylor was in Texas somewhere and was a Southern Baptist school. Unbelievably, I applied, was accepted and was assigned a roommate—all sight unseen. Back then there were no websites to check out. I just thought going to Texas sounded intriguing, so off I went. The curious thing about that is that I sound like quite the adventurer. The truth is, I was definitely not adventurous! It is my belief still today that God oversaw the whole process—my thoughts, my feelings, my spontaneity—as a way of allowing me to meet my future husband.

When I arrived in Texas in August that year, I noticed a few makeshift signs on buildings and along the roads that read, "Yankee Go Home" and "Damn Yankees." I had no clue that these applied to me! It was during the oil embargo, and many northerners had lost their jobs and had headed south to find work. Texans apparently didn't like that too much. Nonetheless, I was excited about my pending future in my new state.

A quick scan of everyone in the dorms netted the conclusion that every coed was a blonde and a former cheerleader. I was neither. I think it was days before I saw another brunette. The blond highlights I was sporting weren't going to cut it. What's more, I definitely needed to grow my hair long. I think I was the only one whose hair length was above my shoulders. The second

College sweethearts. Mike and Kim Singletary met as students at Baylor University. First they were friends, and then a couple. They were married on May 25, 1984. Today they have six children and live in Northern California.

indication that I might be in for trouble was the fact that I clearly didn't get the memo about the coordinating dorm-room accessories. Most of the other rooms were decorated to the nines, complete with matching quilts, rugs and happy window valances. And pink. The entire dorm was a sea of pink. These rooms were more eccentric than the room I had left at home.

Perhaps the most intimidating difference was my northern accent (which, until that point, I never knew I had). When I spoke, I was met with a variety of responses, everywhere from "Where are you from?" to that blank stare that says, "I have no clue what you're saying." All of the external factors screamed at me: "You don't belong here!" In spite of it all, my parents—who had brought me to school—left and, naively, I moved the sinking feeling that I didn't belong to the back of my mind. I was excited about my new adventure.

I joined a group called the Sideline Buddies, where two or three girls were assigned to a football player to bake, decorate and generally cheer for him before each game. It was a great way to get to know some of the players. While a sideline buddy, I caught the eye of number 63, Mike Singletary. He said that he knew he was going to marry me the first moment he saw me. After a few conversations with him, I had him pegged as a dreamer, a big talker and an extremely arrogant jock. He could talk: "I'm going to be the greatest linebacker that Baylor ever had." "I'm going to go pro." "One day, I'll be one of the greatest linebackers that ever played this game." "I knew the moment I saw you that you would be my wife." Every line got the same reaction from me: Riiiight.

The fact that Mike was African-American made a dating relationship impossible—a non-issue. There was not a chance. It wasn't even on my radar screen. What I was OK with, though, was a friendship. Mike and I talked and talked, and we walked and talked some more. I was so different from many of the coeds there, but this didn't seem to matter to him. Actually, he seemed to genuinely enjoy my company.

As my friendship with Mike blossomed, there were some rumblings around campus. Some people reckoned that I was spending too much time with him. I had some girlfriends who cautioned that it "looked bad" for me to be spending so much time with an African American, but in my heart I didn't think much of their warning because Mike and I were just friends.

It was when I went home for the summer after my freshman year that I knew I was in trouble. I dated guys in Michigan but found myself missing Mike. We talked a couple times that summer, but I grew a bit nervous because I was becoming aware of my true feelings for him—and they were more than just friendship feelings. I handled these thoughts the only way I could, with good, old-fashioned denial. When we returned to Baylor for our sophomore year, I didn't think about the future; I simply enjoyed each day with Mike, as friends—but I paid a social price for the time I spent with him.

Before long, Mike was getting national attention as a linebacker and he was becoming Baylor's golden boy. With an NFL career becoming a greater reality for Mike, Baylor wasn't thrilled about having anything stand in the way of that. We both faced pressure from our friends and families to break up.

Finally the pressure worked, at least for a while. The summer after Mike was drafted, we broke up. He was facing the greatest opportunity of his life, and he could really only concentrate on one thing at a time. We were apart for two weeks, and without knowing it, we both agonized over the decision. He sought counsel from his pastor and his coach. I dealt with it alone. I thought about putting my feelings for him aside and choosing the easier route. Our racial differences seemed to be such an issue for so many people. I was miserable without him—but clearly everyone else would be happy if I moved on.

For the first time in my life, I had to make a very tough decision—and I had to do it on my own. Before that point, I had always chosen to take the safe, ripple-free path. Not only would this decision cause ripples, it would stir up tidal waves!

I was the original rule-following, stay-in-the-box, pleaser child. I had fully intended to stay that way for the rest of my life. I figured I'd be safe and predictable forever. Then Mike came along. I was fascinated with his out-of-the-box, structureless, go-for-broke, ridiculously optimistic outlook. He thought big thoughts, made even bigger goals, and dreamed of the impossible. He made the road less traveled look a lot more exciting.

Would I spend the rest of my life being safe? Predictable? Pleasing to others, in spite of my own feelings? I saw this as my greatest decision. Life with Mike, albeit difficult, would be much more exciting. I chose to take the risk on a love that was way out of any box I had ever known.

Twenty years later, looking back at our marriage I see that our road less traveled has often been an off-road experience, and still is to this day. At times, when I gaze at the wider road, the road more traveled, I long for some smooth terrain. If it were up to Mike, we'd never be on a paved road! Fortunately, we chose God's path. It is indeed the narrow path, but together we rolled up our shirtsleeves and decided two things: the narrow path is the one for us and divorce is not an option.

God has provided us with the perfect roadways to bring us to this point. Our Lord has a way of knowing when I need some serious concrete! He also knows when Mike needs the challenges of the rough terrain, like venturing into coaching after a decade of retirement from football. God is our foundation.

Enter by the narrow gate, for the gate is wide, and the way is broad that leads to destruction, and many are those who enter by it. For the gate is small, and the way is narrow that leads to life, and few are those who find it (see Matt. 7: 13-14, *NASB*).

God knew exactly what He was doing when He led me to Baylor. I was not to blend in and I was not to sacrifice the person I was, because He had the road less traveled in store for me. He molded me and shaped me through those experiences to fit on the narrow path. As for our decision never to divorce, I know many people say that, particularly during the honeymoon phase, but we each had a burden for that. He came from a broken home, and I came from a family that had generations of long marriages. Each of us held firmly to our convictions that drove us to that decision—and hold on, we have! I can tell you that I never entertained the thought of splitting up—not even on my worst, most angry days. We've dealt with much over the last 20 years, but through it all we put whatever dilemma we were facing in God's hands. He hasn't always come through the way I thought God should have, especially when He has revealed my flaws and areas for growth. But He has been consistent. He always answers the call.

We are regularly asked, "How do you do it?" How do we manage this life in professional football, and this schedule, with seven kids? We surrender. Just as we surrendered the suggestions of well-meaning people for us to consider an alternative mate; just as Mike surrendered the scouts' expectations for the prototype linebacker; just as I surrendered my plans to have only three or four kids; just as we surrendered our business plan for God to trade it in for a career in coaching. We surrender daily.

Each time Mike and I have surrendered something—together or as individuals—we have received immeasurable blessings. Do I crave a husband who comes home at the same time every day? One who can fill in the gaps in the kids' routine? One who knows at all times where his keys and wallet are? One that will forego discipline and eat a whole box of Girl Scout cookies with me, or even skip a workout? One who is content to take the wide road? Yes, at times, but never for long. This narrow, off-road terrain that we have chosen is far more rewarding, because God is behind the wheel. We're blessed beyond measure.

We both look back on those days at Baylor. They were such difficult, trying times. But I would do it all again in order to receive the relationship I have with Mike today. What a gift those times were. What a gift Mike is to me.

ONE-ON-ONE

A Mother's Prayers

Only because of my mother's prayers and God's grace am I here.

When my mother was pregnant with me, her doctors recommended aborting me. She already had given birth nine times and had had several miscarriages. The doctors predicted that if I were to be born, at best I would be sickly. But my mom knew a "God thing" when she saw one, so she prayed and decided to let God be God.

The doctors were partly right. When I was a kid, it seemed that I always had bronchitis, pneumonia, asthma or some ailment. For years, I would wake up many mornings, go to a hospital (or a clinic) and get a shot—usually a doctor or nurse would examine me, too. I was a regular at the hospital. In fact, I clearly remember the time when I had to sleep in an oxygen tent. The doctors told my mom, "This kid will *not* have a normal childhood. He will have a difficult time keeping up with the others."

Many nights my mom would come to my bedside, rub ointment on my chest and pray for me. She trusted God, and God was faithful. As I began to grow, I became stronger. I remember those days like yesterday.

At first, I played alone in our yard. Sometimes I hung out with my mom. When I was eight or nine, I was strong enough to explore the neighborhood. I would watch other kids play all kinds of sports and sometimes they would let me run races against them. God was answering my mother's prayers.

Before long I wanted to play football. My mother wasn't so sure that I should do that. In addition to being concerned about my physical safety, she also had to overcome our Pentecostal church's stance against playing any kind of sport. I imagine that she talked to God about it, and knowing how she prayed, she likely told Him that she would not go against it as long as it was a God thing.

For they are people blessed by the LORD, and their children, too, will be blessed. I will answer them before they even call to me. While they are still talking to me about their needs, I will go ahead and answer their prayers! (Isa. 65:23-24).

In some ways Mike reminds me of Samuel in the Old Testament. They both became the best at what they did and they both had mothers who really knew how to get God's attention.

Unlike Mike's mom, Samuel's mom, Hannah, had been barren. The lack of a child hurt so much that she bitterly cried out to God, asking Him for a son. She was so emotional in her plea that the priest thought she had been drinking. Hannah wasn't drunk; rather, she was desperate. In her prayer, she promised God that she would give back to Him any son that was born to her. As a sign of commitment, the boy's hair would not be cut for his entire life.[1] God remembered this praying mother's request and gave her a son. It was a God thing.

Hannah named her son Samuel, which sounds like the Hebrew term for "asked of God" or "heard by God."[2] In other words, Samuel was literally an answer to prayer.

Because God kept His word, Hannah kept hers. When Samuel was old enough, she sent him to the high priest who in turn raised him in the things of God. Hannah, like Mike's mom, knew that once she had gotten God's attention, she had to let God be God.

Samuel grew up and became the last judge in the 350-year span of judges who had authority in Israel. Because of Hannah's promise, by the time Samuel led his people to victory over the Philistines he likely had very long hair (unless he was bald by then).[3] Samuel was a legend in his day and a hero for all time. He was a kingmaker and a prototype for all of God's prophets to come.

For Samuel, as it would be for Mike many millennium later, his very existence began with a heartfelt prayer from a faithful mother and the grace of God.

Was someone praying for you before you were born? Are you praying for someone? Have you seen the grace of God at work in your life?

Dear God of Grace, thank You for the loved ones who have prayed for me over the years. I believe that I have come to see You because people have prayed for me. Likewise, please remind me to be faithful in praying for the people You have put in my life. Thank You.

TODAY'S READING: 1 SAMUEL 1:1-28; 2:18-21;
MATTHEW 7:7-12; ROMANS 8:26-30

SINGULETARY

Passion to Play

I didn't just want to play football—*I had to play*. My yearning was so great that if my mother had said no, I was ready to run away from home. That was passion—on my part. The notion of running away was bold for a 12-year-old, but it also was stupid. Thankfully, despite any immature notions we might entertain, God will still allow us to pursue our heart's desires.

At that time, for me, football was life. I loved the game and I latched on to it. I was willing to do whatever it took to play. Not only did I love the game, but early on I also saw it as a way to overcome my tough circumstances.

As a kid, I was often sick. My dad moved out. My mom had to get a job to provide for the last two (of ten) children who were still at home. One time we almost lost our house. Life was not easy. Sometimes it hurt a lot. Out of this pain came an idea.

I was one of those two remaining kids at home, and I began to think, *How can I help? How can I take care of my mom? She deserves better!* Getting a paper route or working at McDonald's might have helped a little but I wanted to help a lot. I knew that before I could make a significant difference I had to be great at something; that something was football. *I just knew it.* Football was an easy choice because having enthusiasm for what we do greatly increases the chances that we can succeed at it.

As I played, I realized that I wanted to be the best. It didn't matter that I'd been sick, that I came from a broken home or that my family was poor. Football came naturally. I didn't have to ask, *Am I committed to this? Do I really want to do it?* My thoughts were more like *Man, I love this game!* I had passion.

Never be lazy in your work, but serve the Lord enthusiastically (Rom. 12:11).

I didn't just want to play basketball—I enjoyed it. But I was lazy. My yearning for the game wavered, sometimes it wobbled, and I was easily distracted by other pursuits. To be honest, my passion for my game was nowhere near as strong as Mike's was for his. Even though I played in an NCAA final-eight game against UCLA and later joined the Los Angeles Lakers, I could have been so much better than I was.

It wasn't until I was in my early 30s that a true fervor emerged. The Lord gave me a passion for souls. I now love to tell people about Jesus! In the Bible we read about Paul. He had this same zeal, but it did not start that way.

This great apostle embodied passion—both the wrong and right kinds. When Paul first came on the scene he was known as Saul, the greatest enemy of the Church. He didn't just hate Christians, he enthusiastically had them killed.[1] *Fox News* would have labeled him a religious extremist and a terrorist.

Saul was there when Stephen was stoned.[2] He was the official witness and was watching the coats of the men who threw rocks at the Church's first martyr. That day a "great wave of persecution" began.[3] Saul enthusiastically participated, going door to door in search of believers. If any were found, they were thrown in jail.[4]

On the road to Damascus, God got Saul's attention.[5] Saul became a believer. His name was changed to Paul and his passion was changed to saving lost souls. He went out immediately and "began preaching about Jesus in the synagogues, saying, 'He is indeed the Son of God!'"[6]

The discovery of my passion was not as dramatic as Paul's, but in the end we shared the same pursuit. Actually, as you will read in a few pages, Mike caught the same passion for souls, too. What about you?

Great God and Savior, help me to have the right kind of passion. Show me the value of a soul and give me a zeal for those whom You have put in my life. Let me be less concerned about my own comfort and more concerned about where others will be spending eternity. Amen.

New Shoes

My mom was born in Waco, Texas. I was born nearby in Houston. Baylor University is in Waco. So my going to Baylor was pretty much set.

One of Baylor's team captains, Ron Barnes, showed me around campus. "You'll be eating here three times a day," he said pointing to the cafeteria. "This is where you'll stay," he said of the dorms.

All I could think was, *How am I going to afford this?* When I sat down with Baylor's head coach, Grant Teaff, I nervously asked, "How much money do I have to spend in order to be here?"

I had no clue what a scholarship was. "Well, Son," the coach replied, "we're offering you a full scholarship. That means your books are free, your room is free, the food that you eat is free and the tuition's free."

I only needed money on Sundays when the cafeteria was closed. Being poor as a church mouse, there were times I didn't eat. Coach Teaff saw my problem and helped me solve it without breaking any rules.

On some Sundays Coach spoke at churches. He took me with him. After one event, he told me about his honorarium and said I would be a good speaker.

After I had spent a few weeks observing Coach speak, he called and asked if I would stand in for him one week. I told him that I would do it, but he could tell that I was petrified.

"Yeah, you've got to go," he said, not backing off one bit. "I need you to do me this favor. Thanks, Mike."

I was sweating. The receiver was even wet. I knew that I could not fill the coach's shoes.

Well, I went and spoke. I was awful; nonetheless, Coach Teaff gave me a few more opportunities. I spoke at the YMCA, the city council, the Fellowship of Christian Athletes and some churches. It was pretty cool to get an honorarium and have some jingle jangle in my pocket. It was even better to know that I had a coach who cared about me as a person, not just as a player.

> When they reached the other side, Elijah said to Elisha, "What can I do for you before I'm taken from you? Ask anything." Elisha said, "Your life repeated in my life. I want to be a holy man just like you" (2 Kings 2:9, *THE MESSAGE*).

Coach Teaff knew Mike didn't have enough money to eat out when the Baylor cafeteria was closed. But as coach he also knew the NCAA rules: Neither coaches nor alumni could give players money, not even a few dollars a week for food.

Instead of leaving his young linebacker with an empty stomach, the coach lived out an old saying: *Give a man a fish and you feed him for a day. Teach him how to fish and he can feed himself for a lifetime.* When Coach Teaff taught Mike how to speak, he taught him how to fish. And he also taught his protégé how to wear new shoes.

The Bible is packed with similar stories of people caring, nurturing, teaching, training and coaching others. Such actions can be called mentoring or discipleship. Elijah was one of the best disciplers.

God sent Elijah on a recruiting trip.[1] Elijah found Elisha and threw his mantle over the young man's shoulders. They both knew what this meant. In a way, it was like receiving a scholarship. God not only wanted Elisha to be on the team, but He also wanted the young boy to fill the shoes of the prophet.

Elijah is one of two people in the Bible who never died; he was caught up in a whirlwind instead.[2] After discipling Elisha and before leaving this world, Elijah granted his protégé one last wish. The young disciple surprised his mentor by asking for a double portion of the old man's spirit.[3]

When Elijah was whisked away, Elisha picked up the old man's mantle and got the double portion. When he parted the Jordan River, he saw that his new shoes were a good fit. Elijah had done his job. He had prepared a man to follow in his footsteps.[4]

Are you an Elijah or an Elisha? Being an Elijah can start with an act as simple as teaching a man to fish—or speak. Being an Elisha can start with an act as simple as saying yes to filling in for a coach or wishing for a double portion.

Heavenly Father, lead me to the person You want to disciple me
[lead me to the person You want me to disciple]. I don't want to stay
in the same place with You any longer. I'm tired of that.
I want to grow spiritually. I want new shoes.

TODAY'S READING: 1 KINGS 19:19-21; 2 KINGS 2:1-15;
LUKE 14:25-33; HEBREWS 11:5-6

A Lighter Load

Making the decision to go to Baylor was the easy part. Actually going there was harder. When my family dropped me off at school I cried, thinking *I can't let them down. I can't allow myself to fail.*

I wanted to succeed—mostly for my mom, I suppose. I had a brother who had gone to jail, sisters who had had babies out of wedlock and before my dad had walked out, parents who fought like cats and dogs. Despite the tough circumstances, I always believed the Singletary name was supposed to be special. I decided, *I'm going to take this name out of the mess that it's in and put it where it belongs. I'm going to represent this name. It will one day stand for character, pride and integrity.* Those were weighty ambitions for an 18-year-old. I carried a lot of self-imposed pressure.

At that time in my life God wasn't much more than a Santa Claus to me. I trusted Him, but not completely. I didn't serve Him. I made up a lot of my own rules. I just asked for stuff. So when it came to actually living out my dream, I tried to do it all alone—but the load was so heavy.

The huge amount of pressure was most intense on game day. I got really revved up. I would hyperventilate and build up a rapid heart rate. While everyone else listened to rock, rap and hip-hop to amp up, I would listen to Beethoven to try to calm down. I started to ride a stationary bicycle before the game and when the offense was on the field. I worked on taking breaths between plays. Nothing helped. After months of trying to calm down, I gave up. I thought, *OK, I'll just be Mike Singletary and I'll carry the weight.* That's the way I played—like a man under pressure who would explode on game day.

I wish I'd trusted God with my burdens a lot earlier than I did. Once I turned everything over to Him, my load was lightened and I became a much better player.

Then Jesus said, "Come to me, all of you who are weary and carry heavy burdens, and I will give you rest. Take my yoke upon you. Let me teach you, because I am humble and gentle, and you will find rest for your souls. For my yoke fits perfectly, and the burden I give you is light" *(Matt. 11:28-30).*

Have you ever lugged a heavy suitcase through a busy airport? Having all of the weight on one side of your body or the other, switching hands and constantly dropping the suitcase is exhausting. Put some wheels on it and everything changes.

When it comes to burdens, God serves as the wheels. He rarely carries the entire load—we wouldn't learn if He did—but He does make carrying our loads more bearable. For an illustration from the Bible, we again turn to Elijah. The prophet knew God would help him, but sometimes he tried to lug the suitcase through the airport by himself anyway.

Elijah stood before kings proclaiming the Word of the Lord, and he did so without fear. God even made him a victor over 850 false prophets.[1]

But one day, right after his victory on Mount Carmel, Elijah was spent. He let threats from a cruel queen named Jezebel get to him.[2] Elijah took the wheels off his suitcase and dragged it into the desert. He felt alone and discouraged. God met him there and perked him up, but Elijah had removed the wheels once too often. After anointing a couple of kings, it was time to anoint his successor, Elisha.[3]

Before we fully trusted God, neither Mike nor I understood His desire to help us. Even in his maturity, Elijah sometimes forgot. We all carried more weight than was necessary. Mike and I were young and lacked understanding, so God cut us some slack. He certainly did the same for Elijah when he was young. But when Elijah was confronted by Jezebel and again removed his wheels, God flexed a firm hand. Elijah was too mature in his faith to get away with such behavior. He did not lose his honor, but his service was over.

If you are new in the faith, put the wheels on your suitcase. If you are mature in the faith, don't dare take them off. Not only will your load be lighter but you will be able to take your suitcase further.

All Powerful Bearer of Burdens, thank You for being the wheels that allow me to cope with the weight of life. Great God, I want to lean on You for understanding. Guard me from the foolishness of usurping Your role and trying to go it alone. I want to walk with You.

The Right Time to Pray

Coming out of college, I saw myself following in the footsteps of great linebackers such as Dick Butkus, Willie Lanier and Lee Roy Jordan. I had played well at Baylor and expected an NFL team to draft me in the first round. Not everyone saw it that way. The Oakland Raiders' scout said, "Mike, I really like the way you play, but you're just not big enough. We like our linebackers big."

Others echoed this sentiment. One scout came to a workout looking for me. He hollered, "Hey, where's Mike Singletary?"

I said, "This is me."

"You're not the guy I saw on film," he stammered. "You can't be."

"Yes, Sir. That's who I am."

Disbelieving, he asked the trainer, "Is this Mike Singletary?"

The trainer said, "Yeah."

"Wow! Small guy," the scout exclaimed. "I thought you were bigger than that."

That's the story of my life. Scouts from the Seahawks, Chargers and Chiefs responded the same way.

The Chicago Bears were different. "Mike," their scout began, "we really like you. We like you a lot. You remind us of the way Dick Butkus played."

I said, "I'll make you forget about Dick Butkus." (Butkus was a Hall of Famer and had played for the Bears.)

He said, "Well, if you're there in the second round—"

"See you're talking wrong now," I interrupted. "I won't be there in the second round. I'll be gone."

Draft day came and I was expecting to be taken somewhere in the middle to the end of the first round. But it didn't happen. After the first-round picks were complete and no team had selected me, I went outside angry, disturbed and disappointed. I vented; then I prayed, "Lord, if You want me to play, let me play for the Chicago Bears." About five seconds later, my girlfriend (who is now my wife) and my mom came outside all excited: "Mike! The Bears just traded some picks and they just drafted you." The timing was incredible. My prayer was answered in five seconds.

Your Father knows exactly what you need even before you ask him! (Matt. 6:8).

As it turned out, Mike didn't make everyone forget Dick Butkus, but he did give them another name to remember. Mike had the goods and proved it on the field. After a long career with the Chicago Bears, he too was inducted into the NFL Hall of Fame and was named one of *Sporting News*'s all-time top 100 NFL players.

Of course, on draft day, no one knew how good Mike would be; Mike was the only one who believed he would be one of the game's best. Mike's mistake was having too much confidence in himself and not enough confidence in God. In this situation, the lesson wasn't even so much about pride or ego. It had more to do with the timing of a prayer and trusting God.

Mike turned to God midstream, only after his own plan fell flat. If he'd prayed first he would have gone into draft day with the confidence of knowing that whatever happened was God's will rather than relying only on his own athletic abilities and charisma.

We all do what Mike did. We charge into situations in our own strength, instead of praying and enlisting God's hand from the get-go. That is not too smart on our part because God knows what we need before we ask.[1] In other words, He has a plan. And that plan is better than any strategy we can devise.

Was God's original plan for Mike to be a Bear? That is not the point here. Rather, I am pointing out that God certainly would have preferred Mike go through draft day with the peace of mind that comes when we know that *there is a plan*.

Since God wants to do more for us than we can think or ask,[2] why wait until our plans collapse before turning to Him? If we ask according to God's will, He is eager to give us good gifts.[3] That means that if we ask first, we are in a much better position to know God's will, and we will usually save ourselves a lot of grief, too.

Great God of the Perfect Plan, I want to remember to get You
involved from the beginning of everything I do. And I want
everything I do to be what You want done. Lord, I want to be in
Your perfect will, to the glory of Your Son, Jesus Christ. Amen.

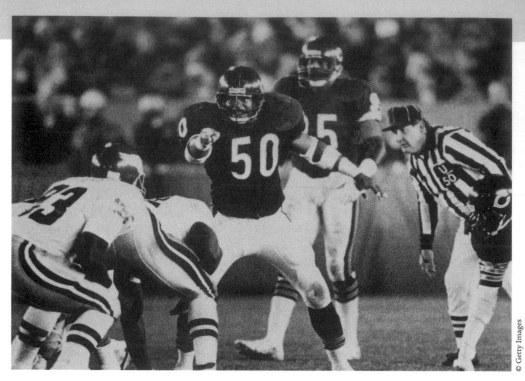

A Defensive Presence. Opposing quarterbacks always knew when Mike Singletary was in the game. When number 50 (above) did not sack them, he intimidated them. On the sidelines (below), Mike uses headphones to plot out a defensive strategy with Bears' coaches in the booth. Mike even made the cover of Sports Illustrated (below, right).

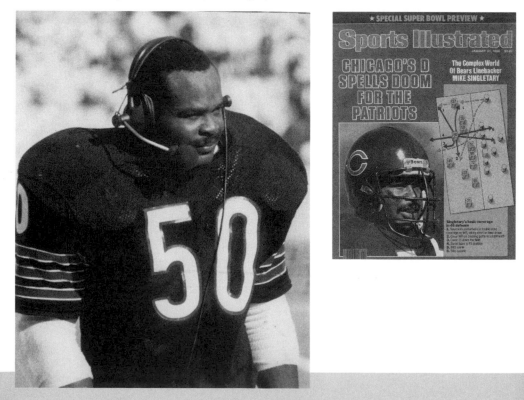

Intensity. Mike always gave 100 percent, whether in the game (above) or working out with fellow Bear, the late Walter Payton (number 34), during a minicamp in 1987 (below).

Knock, Knock

During my first year with the Bears, our defensive coordinator, Buddy Ryan, wouldn't play me in our nickel defense on third and long. I asked him what I needed to do to play every down. Buddy said, "Don't even think about it because we don't have middle linebackers play the nickel."

I said, "But I can play it. What do I need to do to play on the nickel defense?"

He looked at me and said, "All right. I'll tell you what. You go home this off-season and get down to 225 pounds [I weighed 245 pounds]. You've got to be able to run with the deep receivers not just the running backs."

Buddy Ryan is one of the all-time great coaches. He knew what he was talking about. Buddy told me that if I wanted to play the nickel defense, I would need to know the whole defense, not just the linebacker position. He added that even if I did all he had asked, I still would not be able to practice the nickel defense, because he was not going to take time away from other players.

I was not deterred. The next summer, I went into camp at 225. I had watched a lot of film and worked with our defensive backs on the coverage and footwork. Buddy was not deterred either. He said, "Son, I don't know why you keep doing this stuff. You're not going to play on the nickel defense."

One day we were playing the Detroit Lions. My teammate Otis Wilson got hurt but the second-string nickel guy wasn't ready, so I jumped off the bench and ran into the game.

"Where you going?" Buddy asked.

"We don't have a lot of time. Give me the call real quick," I said, not blinking once.

Buddy was cursing under his breath, but he gave me the call. I played the rest of the game and after that, I always played the nickel.

And so I tell you, keep on asking, and you will be given what you ask for. Keep on looking, and you will find. Keep on knocking, and the door will be opened. For everyone who asks, receives. Everyone who seeks, finds. And the door is opened to everyone who knocks (Luke 11:9-10).

Mike was unrelenting. He pestered his coach and got to play the nickel. There is a spiritual principle here. In God's game plan, persistence, specifically constantly coming to Him through prayer, seems to be crucial. The 12 disciples made this discovery early on when they watched Jesus pray.

The Son of God stayed in touch with His Father almost constantly. Jesus prayed at His baptism, during His temptation, on retreat up on a mountain, when alone and sometimes all night long. Jesus was prayerfully persistent. His disciples noticed and requested, "Lord, teach us to pray."[1]

In response, Jesus gave them the Lord's Prayer. It wasn't meant to be prayed over and over again. Repetition isn't the same as persistence. Jesus taught against vain repetition.[2] This disciples guide to prayer (a more accurate title) was to be a model for building prayers. Jesus didn't say, "Repeat these words." He said, "Pray in this way."[3]

Jesus outlined seven points through which we are to pray: adoration, God's will, needs, confession, guidance, spiritual warfare and God's glory. In addition to praying for our own needs, we are to use these points as we pray for nations, rulers, enemies and friends. Using parables, the Son of God further demonstrated how this works. He recommended pestering persistence and constant coming.

In one parable, Jesus tells the story of a midnight run to a neighbor's house in search of bread. (Obviously there were no 7-Elevens back then.) Jesus tells a crowd, "If you keep knocking [at your neighbor's door] long enough, he [your neighbor] will get up and give you what you want so his reputation won't be damaged."[4]

In short, if we are persistent in coming to God, we can expect our prayers to be answered. When it comes to God's business, if we want to get off the bench and get into the game, nonchalance won't cut it. God wants us to pray with purpose, intensity and longevity. He wants us to keep knocking.

Almighty Author of Prayer, show me Your will. I want Your will to be my will. Show me how to pray Your will constantly and persistently. I don't want to sit on the bench any longer. Lord, teach me to pray! Thank You.

TODAY'S READING: PSALM 91:15; ISAIAH 65:24; JEREMIAH 33:3; MATTHEW 6:5-15; LUKE 11:1-11; 18:1-8; JOHN 15:7

Playing on the Bears' defense was like playing outfield for the New York Yankees or point guard for the Los Angeles Lakers. Like the Yankees and the Lakers, the Bears have a long and storied tradition of winning.

Over 12 seasons, in the 1930s and 1940s, Chicago claimed 4 NFL titles and 7 division championships. Led by the legendary Bronko Nagurski, those Bears became the Monsters of the Midway.[1]

Dick Butkus was another Monster of the Midway. Beginning in the mid-1960s, he led the Chicago defense, averaging an incredible 120 tackles and 58 assists a year for 8 years.

When I arrived in the Windy City in 1981, Butkus had been retired for eight years and the Bears were struggling. In 1984, we had lost most of our linebackers to injury. We were desperate. Buddy Ryan, a football genius and our defensive coordinator, watched a lot of film, tinkered and asked questions. Then he concocted something new: He designed what became known as the 46 defense.

In this defensive scheme, Buddy put four men on the line of scrimmage, six defensive backs close to the line and one safety roaming the field. Normally, four guys rush. With the 46, our opponents now had to worry about eight or nine guys rushing on every down.

Having eight or nine defensive players crowding the line creates a lot of pressure. Normally on each play an offense will send five people down field on pass routes. But those five aren't going to leave the line of scrimmage open to nine opposing rushers. Somebody's got to block and protect the quarterback.

There was a twist to our defense: Not only did we have nine rushers but also an opposing offense never knew which nine Bears would be rushing. We had guy's jumping in and out, racing forward from 10 yards back. The opposing quarterback had three seconds before we would smack him. We could see panic in the eyes of the other guys. It was out-of-the-box crazy. With the 46, we again became the Monsters of the Midway and won a Super Bowl.

But Jesus told him, "Follow me now! Let those who are spiritually dead care for their own dead" (Matt. 8:22).

The Bears were in trouble. Injuries had decimated the linebacking corps. Only Mike Singletary was healthy. Necessity required some innovative thinking. In response, Buddy Ryan talked to his guys. He looked in their eyes and searched for fear or hesitation. He wanted to know who needed help and who didn't as he designed a defense around the players he had. He wanted people who would not hesitate to play out of the box.

Buddy had 11 defensive players on the football field. Jesus started with 12 on His team. When Jesus came along with His out-of-the-box thinking, 11 of the 12 didn't balk—they dropped what they were doing to follow Him. However, there were differences in the ways Jesus' men came. Those who had been fishermen left their catches that day, but they retained their gear. They kept their boats registered in their names and their nets folded nearby. When they followed Jesus, they *dropped* the work of the day but they didn't immediately *give up* everything. For the fishermen, giving up everything would take some time. In sharp contrast, the tax collector Matthew dropped his business of the day *and* gave his all to Jesus. When Buddy Ryan was putting together his new defense, he needed people who had the no-hesitation, can do attitude that Matthew modeled.

Matthew had been hated. Tax collectors were considered to be traitorous scum and were despised more than used-chariot salesmen. When Matthew stood up and followed Jesus, he walked away from everything—including his job. His was the boldest response. Perhaps that's why he got to write one of the gospels.

In life, each of us will face times when we are called upon to think in a new way or to turn in a new direction. How do we respond when God—the greatest out-of-the-box thinker of all—is doing the calling? How do we react when others hesitate? Do we give up whatever is on our mind at the moment? Do we lay down all we are? Do we seek an escape hatch or do we eagerly follow?

Gracious Lord, I don't want to hesitate or give an excuse when You call me. I want You to show me how to balance my roles with my family, friends, church and community and still place You first. I don't want to say no to You in any way. I want to follow Jesus.

TODAY'S READING: MATTHEW 8:18-22; LUKE 9:23-27; 57—62;
PHILIPPIANS 2:5-11; JAMES 5:1-12

The Extra Mile

Buddy Ryan taught me his defense. From him I learned how to blitz and how to read the opposing team's next play. Buddy showed me signs to look for, such as the direction of the quarterback's eyes, the guard turning his foot and the blocking back leaning in a particular direction. I started going to his office on my days off to watch film with him. I wouldn't say a word and he wouldn't say a word. We just sat there watching film of our games and of other games. Every now and then he'd take his pipe out of his mouth and say, "See that play?"

I'd say, "Yes."

Then he'd put the pipe back in his mouth, and we'd watch more film. Eventually he'd take the pipe out again and ask, "Think you can cover that guy?"

It didn't take too long before I had a feel for the upcoming game. After a while I would go to Buddy's office, get a blank game plan, go home and look at film by myself—I tried to see in the film what Buddy saw. I'd write out what I thought the defense should be and I'd bring it back to him. Some calls I'd be right on and other calls I'd be way off. But he allowed me to do that and began to explain what to look for and how to find weaknesses. Over time, we formed a strong relationship.

One night Buddy said, "Singletary, I've got to go home."

"Go ahead and go, Coach," I said. "I'm staying here. I've got to work. I've got to study."

It became a routine. I would go in early in the morning and leave late at night. I would go in on my days off. I was the guy with the film projector (those were the days before DVDs and laptop computers). When we traveled, I took the projector and put it in my room. I was always watching film. I was always studying how to play better. Buddy had taught me how, and then some.

As Samuel grew up, the LORD was with him, and everything Samuel said was wise and helpful. All the people of Israel from one end of the land to the other knew that Samuel was confirmed as a prophet of the LORD (1 Sam. 3:19-20).

Buddy Ryan went from bringing the rookie off the bench into the game, to starting him, to playing him on every down, and finally, to letting him do his own play calling. Buddy gave Mike progressive freedom because Mike took the time to learn the ropes, and then some.

The better we get at what we do, the more freedom we get to do it. Progressive freedom is the outcome of "and then some." Samuel is a good illustration of this principle.

Samuel was raised as a temple kid. His mom had kept her promise to the Lord and had given him to the High Priest to be raised in the ways of worship.[1]

Eli was in charge but he was a terrible High Priest because he was a really bad dad. His two boys were getting rich from stealing offerings and were abusing their authority by molesting young women. By the time Eli decided to do something about it, he was too old and had lost his clout—his boys had overrun his authority. God cursed them for their rebellion and sacrilege.

Samuel did not take up the acts of Eli's boys; nonetheless, he was raised in a highly conflicted environment. Samuel thrived because of his attitude. He served as Eli's helper,[2] opened the temple doors[3] and probably assisted the high priest with offerings. Samuel was like a son to Eli but remained separate and listened to his Heavenly Father. After Samuel learned the ropes, and then some, God confirmed him as a prophet. The process was progressive freedom.

Serving others by doing ordinary tasks is serving God. Every job has dignity, because ultimately the one we serve is God. So when we do our tasks, and then some, we are going the extra mile for God. Blessings don't come from seeking blessings. Blessings come from doing "and then some" as an act of worship. Progressive freedom will be one of the results.

Are you ready to go the extra mile, and then some?

Dear God of the Extra Mile, You solved the problem of my sin. Thank You.
Show me ways to demonstrate my gratitude. I want to go the extra mile for
You. And thank You for my progressive freedom in Christ. May I honor
You with it and not turn it into cheap grace. Amen.

TODAY'S READING: 1 SAMUEL 2:18-36; 3:1-21; ROMANS 6:12—7:7

In horse racing jargon, Buddy Ryan gave me my head, but he held on to the reins. Buddy told me, "I know you study and I know how hard you work. I know you know what I want. When you're on the field, if you feel or see something, you call it. If you're wrong, I'm going to get on you in front of the other coaches and the team, because that's my job."

Buddy walked an interesting tight rope because he had an issue with the other coaches. As the defensive coordinator, they felt that Buddy ought to make all the calls. The success or failure of the defense often meant the difference between winning and losing. Of course, winning and losing made the difference between keeping and losing jobs. The other coaches didn't want their jobs resting on me. They didn't like the idea of doing a lot of preparation and planning, and then giving me impromptu on-the-field authority that could override everything.

Buddy understood and told me, "If you make a bad call, just know that I have to get on you about it. But also know that it's for show and I trust you with your decisions. Can you handle that?"

There were times when an opposing offense would give us a set we hadn't practiced. Since I knew what Buddy would want, I'd make the adjustment on the spot. This would keep us from having to waste a time-out to get it right.

In all honesty, it didn't make too much difference what play was called, as long as it wasn't a blitz. What mattered is how the play was called. If my teammates saw me as confident, they in turn would be confident. If they weren't worrying about my call being the right call, they would execute it. On the other hand, if I was indecisive, my teammates' execution would be indecisive.

As we know Jesus better, his divine power gives us everything we need for living a godly life. He has called us to receive his own glory and goodness! (2 Pet. 1:3).

Buddy Ryan set the ground rules, gave Mike the basics and devised the game plan. But Buddy didn't cover all the contingencies. They both knew that they would face unexpected situations in a game. So, when variations occurred, it was up to Mike to instantaneously react. Mike needed to know Buddy well enough to know and then do what Buddy would do in whatever situation occurred.

God has given us all we need to be successful in the game of life.[1] The Bible contains the ground rules, the basics and the game plan. It's our job to study this playbook and prepare for the options that the opposition will throw at us.

The Bible doesn't tell us specifics such as when to turn off the television, which magazines to buy and whether or not to go to a certain movie. It's silent on the specifics of playing cards, social dancing and the exact length a dress should be. The Bible does categorically call certain things sin and clearly defines excesses, but God leaves the fuzzy gray areas up to our judgment. The key here is to know Him well enough that we'll do what Jesus would do.

I was at a party where there were two punch bowls: One was labeled "Law" and the other "Grace." The first was straight punch. The second contained alcohol. I don't think Jesus would have cared about having two punch bowls, but I think He would not have liked people poking fun at restraint and flaunting liberty. The problem wasn't the punch bowls. The problem was with the hosts not knowing what Jesus would do.

God expects us to improvise when we come up against something for which we haven't prepared. But He expects us to know Him well enough that we will automatically do what Jesus would do.

Dear Author of Life, I want desperately to live the life that You have given me. I want to constantly measure everything that I do and ask the question, What would Jesus do? Give me the courage and conviction to follow through on this commitment. Thank You.

TODAY'S READING: 2 PETER 1:1-11; TITUS 2:11-14; 1 JOHN 3:13—4:6

Spies

Any good strategy includes espionage. In football, we have spies. If we know what play the other guys are going to run, we can beat it almost every time. We want an edge, but so does our opponent. It is a little bit like a game of chess.

Some teams have people watching the game live on television or sitting at various spots in the stadium with high-powered binoculars. These undercover operatives try to pick up signals from the opposing team so that they can convey the next play to their own coaches.

On the sidelines, coaches cover their mouths or have someone stand in front of them when they talk in an attempt to hide their signals and prevent the opposition from reading their lips. Sometimes I was the guy who would shield our coach. I would just stand there smiling—sometimes I would scowl.

We had hand signals, too. As in baseball, we would go through a series of gestures, but only one would mean anything. The trick was to figure out which motion went with which play. Sometimes the entire set of signals meant nothing at all. Any attempt to decipher it was futile.

Sometimes we would mix the signals in an attempt to confuse our opponent. One particular hand motion simply meant "automatic call." When Buddy Ryan gave this gesture, it meant that I was to make the call, depending upon the opposing team's offensive setup. On those plays, even the highest-powered binoculars in the world would not help the other team because the signal itself meant nothing except "You make the call." The opposing spies could have had our playbook but it would not have helped them unscramble our next defensive play.

Our 46 defense worked much the same way. We camouflaged which of our players would rush our opponent's line. This kept the other team off balance and allowed us to frequently take down their quarterback by surprise. We worked hard at out-strategizing our gridiron enemies. And most of the time, it worked out well.

Be careful! Watch out for attacks from the Devil, your great enemy. He prowls around like a roaring lion, looking for some victim to devour (1 Pet. 5:8).

In sports, our opponents are really not our enemies—just foes that we want to beat. In life, however, we have a real enemy who not only wants to see us lose but who also wants us to score points for his team. Our enemy is the devil (aka Satan) and he is the master of deception.[1] He is the father of lies, and yes, he has spies.

Satan hates God and despises us because we are made in God's image. He doesn't want to spend eternity with us, but neither does he want us spending it with God. He twists the truth, perverts what is good and attempts to take advantage of our weaknesses. He'll do everything he can to keep us off balance. His teammates, the demons who abandoned God along with him, long before Adam and Eve were created, are experts at deception, too.[2]

Satan leads supernatural forces of evil in the heavenly realms with the sole intention of devouring us.[3] He is not omnipresent and his demons cannot read our minds, but he does roam about Earth watching everything that is going on.[4] At least once, Satan even reported back to God, making accusations against Job.[5] However, God, who is omnipresent and does not need spies, already knew everything about Job. After all, God has the hairs on our head counted and knows the desires of our heart.

Satan's strategy is not for him to win he has read the end of the book and knows that he finishes last in the standings. His aim is for us to finish last, too. We will be tested (as Job was). Our job is to be vigilant and humble, and to stand firm.[6] When we put on the whole armor of God,[7] the power of His Word is activated in our lives. Remember, greater is He who is in us than he who is in the world.[8] Simply put, Satan can have all the spies He wants, but when we follow God's strategy we will outwit and overcome our enemies' schemes.

All Powerful God, I want to learn Your Word and be able to stand firm so that the power of Scripture will be cause to make the devil flee. I want all of Your armor. In Jesus' name I pray. Amen.

TODAY'S READING: JOB 1:6-12; ISAIAH 14:12-28;
EPHESIANS 6:10-17; 1 PETER 5:8-10

The Cutback

I had a great season in 1983 and made it to the Pro Bowl for the first time. I was fast, hit hard and was starting to build a reputation as one of the best linebackers in the league. Before the Pro Bowl, Buddy Ryan told me, "Be ready. This coming year opposing coaches will have had all summer to figure out how to throw the kitchen sink at you." At the time, I didn't know what he was talking about—but I found out soon enough.

The kitchen sink turned out to be an offensive technique called the cutback. Not too far into the 1984 season, I realized that I was missing certain plays. I could not make the tackle when the runner was cutting back across the field, and by the time I turned around to go the other direction, an opposing player was there to hit me. *What is this?* I thought. *How are they getting to me?*

Buddy smiled and said, "You've got to respond, not react. They're setting you up because you're too fast. They're using your quickness and reaction speed against you. So, now you've got to slow down and you've got to really read the linemen, read their angles and read the play."

I had to adjust how I played, but once I figured out how to respond rather than react to the cutback I was an even better player. In fact, I was better able to read all of the plays, and I became a complete linebacker.

Now, as a coach, I want my players to respond, not react. If they react, instincts win out over comprehension. They'll get sucked into the play and trapped by their reactions. When they respond, understanding directs their movement. If they react, it means that they have not thought about it much. They can't really see where the play is going. All they know is where they think it's going. But if they slow down a step and take it all in, they'll know what's coming.

"My thoughts are completely different from yours," says the LORD. "And my ways are far beyond anything you could imagine" (Isa. 55:8).

I'm trapped in a snowstorm. My reaction is to walk to safety. However, since I know I can't trust my reactions, I pause for a moment to consider the situation. Like everyone, I have one leg that is slightly shorter than the other. Without a frame of reference I'll walk in a circle. If I go looking for safety, the only thing I'll find will be my own footprints. After thinking it through, rather than racing off in search of help, I respond by digging a snow cave instead—and I wait for help to arrive.

We can't trust our reactions or our first thoughts because our hearts are deceitful and desperately wicked.[1] Our ways are not like God's ways.[2] There is a way that seems as if it is right to us but it winds up in destruction.[3] Our natural reaction is usually the opposite of what God wants. We have to learn to respond.

An airline pilot once told me an interesting story about flying in clouds and fog. I had heard that a plane could be in a slow spiraling descent and the pilot wouldn't know it. This pilot told me that dominant, decisive people have the most difficult time in such situations. Their instincts tell them one thing while the instruments tell them another. They swear that they are flying straight and level. However, the console says the plane is in a 15-degree dive and is veering to the right. Should these pilots trust their instincts or the console? The pilots who survive trust the gauges.

God gave us His instruments. It's His collection of 66 books in the Bible. Our job is to control our reactions in the flesh and respond to the leading of the Spirit through our knowledge of the Word. It takes a moment longer to respond to the Spirit, but it keeps us from walking in circles or from crashing.

Gracious Author of Ultimate Truth, thank You for providing a means for controlling my deceitful heart. Would You lead me to be a responder, instead of a reactor, through the power of Your Holy Spirit? I want to do what's right and glorify Your name. Amen.

TODAY'S READING: PROVERBS 14:12; ISAIAH 55:6—56:5; JEREMIAH 17:9-10; ROMANS 11:33—12:2

SINGLETARY

It was a perfect showdown. The Los Angeles Raiders were the reigning Super Bowl champions, and they were tough, confident. We were a team on the rise, but nobody knew how close we were to being great. The game was in Chicago (in 1984) and it had been built up as a confrontation between two very physical teams.

The first quarter was like a championship-boxing bout. We shadow-boxed a little bit. They hit us, and we jabbed back. We had them against the ropes. They swung hard and bounced back.

We could not play the 46 defense every down of every game or it would not be much of a surprise. If we wanted to ambush our opponent we would have to spring our defense on them. Against the Raiders, we waited until the right moment. When we switched to the 46 we started landing all of our punches. We knocked out Mark Wilson, the Raiders' starting quarterback. They sent in another quarterback. We knocked him out, too. The last quarterback was their punter, Ray Guy. We won, 17-6.

Before the game, our coach, Mike Ditka, had told us, "We've beaten some teams that aren't very good. We need to beat a good team. If we can beat this team, then we'll know who we are."

It was a huge win. It raised the bar and set a new standard for us. We had beaten an elite team. We had ambushed the defending Super Bowl champions. It was pivotal. It was like a big brother coming home from college expecting to impress his younger brother, but while big brother was away, the younger brother had developed some impressive skills of his own. Though it would be another year before we made it to the Super Bowl, when we beat the Raiders, we celebrated like we were the champions.

Those who fight against the LORD will be broken. He thunders against them from heaven; the LORD judges throughout the earth. He gives mighty strength to his king; he increases the might of his anointed one (1 Sam. 2:10).

There is no better Bible story about a little brother showing his big brothers a thing or two than the story of David. God told His prophet Samuel to fill a ram's horn with oil, go to Bethlehem and make a sacrifice to the Lord. Samuel was to invite Jesse and his sons to go along so that he could anoint one of Jesse's boys as the next king.

Jesse brought seven of his eight sons to the event. David was the eighth, but the family left him tending sheep. Jesse didn't think meeting Samuel was a big enough deal to pull his youngest kid away.

Jesse's seven sons walked in according to age, from the oldest to the youngest. Who would be king looked like a no-brainer when the eldest walked in. *He has the look,* Samuel surely thought. But God said no to him and no to the other six.

"There is one more," Jesse stated as an afterthought. "But I doubt if you'll be interested in him. He's ruddy, not regal."[1] To Jesse's surprise, David was anointed as king.

It is not clear how much time passed, but David was again treated like a red-headed stepchild. The three oldest brothers were serving in Saul's army, so Jesse sent David to the front lines with supplies for his boys.

David's oldest brother, Eliab, yelled, "What are you doing here? Why aren't you minding your own business, tending that scrawny flock of sheep? I know what you're up to. You've come down here to see the sights, hoping for a ringside seat at a bloody battle!"[2] He didn't thank David for the food, but rather, he bad-mouthed him because his little brother got anointed and he didn't.

Some time later David killed Goliath. Everyone but David was surprised. Little brother had a lot more going for him than his family members thought. Two groups were silenced that day: the Philistines and David's brothers.

If the Lord's hand of blessing is on someone, join—don't fight—that person, regardless of his or her age or station in life. It's never a good idea to go up against God's anointed.

Heavenly Anointer, help me to be content with my calling and not covet another person's anointing. Show me those whom I should come alongside and support. Help me to be about my Father's business and not concern myself with what I don't have. Teach me to stay focused on what I do have. I pray this for Your honor and glory, not mine. Amen.

Blind to Compassion

Everyone respected coach Tom Landry. He was a winner both on and off the field. While I always wanted to win against his Dallas Cowboys teams, it was just an honor to play against him. If we beat one of his teams, we knew that we had beaten one of the best.

In 1985, we played the Cowboys in Texas. They had long been an elite team and went into the game with a 7-3 record. Most people thought that the Bears were blue-collar trash talkers who were not classy enough to win a Super Bowl. The Cowboys, some said, would show us how the game was supposed to be played.

Our coach, Mike Ditka, was excited about going up against the Cowboys, but he also wanted us to show respect to Landry. Before the game, in response to reporters' questions, instead of dishing out verbal jabs, we said things like "They are America's team"; "It's going to be a tough game"; and "We'll just have to let the best team win."

The game was not even close. We beat them like a drum, 44-0. In the fourth quarter Cowboy quarterback Danny White was bleeding from his lip and nose. He was stumbling to the line of scrimmage, and we were barking like dogs, "I'm gonna get him. I'm gonna get him!"

We were focused, and we had no respect for our elders. We let everybody know that we were the Bears. Finally, I begged our linemen, "Come on. Don't hit him like that any more." White was a gutsy player, but by this point in the game, he was a mess.

I'm intense but not mean-spirited. I always wanted to make a statement when I played and always gave a one-hundred-percent effort. I suppose that is why they called me Samurai Mike. But there is a time for pounding the other team and there is a time for compassion. Danny White is a good guy. We needed to let up and finish the game. Dallas had lost big and they had a lot of wounds to lick.

> But I say, love your enemies! Pray for those who persecute you! In that way, you will be acting as true children of your Father in heaven. For he gives his sunlight to both the evil and the good, and he sends rain on the just and on the unjust, too (Matt. 5:44-45).

When the score is 44-0, the passion to win can blind a team. Thankfully, in the Dallas game, Mike saw when compassion was needed.

A passion to win is not the only emotion that can blind us from the need to show mercy. Other emotions can divert us, too. I once saw two guys on a motorcycle driving down a Southern California freeway. They were wearing only helmets, T-shirts, shorts and sneakers. They must have been zipping along at 85 miles an hour when the bike drifted into another lane, bumped a truck, wobbled and went down. The truck and trailer jack-knifed.

The bike riders miraculously got up off of the pavement and staggered to the side of the road. Traffic had stopped and I was the first person to get to them. Expecting to perform triage, I was surprised when I discovered that neither had life-threatening injuries. They had lost a lot of skin and one had a broken nose, but neither was going to die. When I realized this, my compassion turned to anger because they both reeked of alcohol.

These two drunks had jeopardized lives! Their actions repulsed me. Then I again noticed their pain. I've seen pealed grapes with more skin on them than these guys had. I had almost allowed my anger to blind me but, thankfully, my compassion returned.

The story of the Good Samaritan is well known.[1] Anyone who went to Sunday School knows what went down on that day in Jericho. A visitor from another hood wasn't wearing the right colors (or whatever the equivalent was back then), so a gang mugged him and left him half dead. Passersby avoided the scene, each with their own excuse—each blinded to the need for compassion.

The Greek verb *splanchnizomai* is often translated in the New Testament as "to have compassion," which means to be moved in the inner body parts, intestines or the womb.[2] When the Good Samaritan came upon the man who had been mugged, he showed compassion, bandaged him and helped him on his way.

Jesus told us to go and do likewise.[3]

> *Gracious and Compassionate God, forgive me for the times I've*
> *responded to people in anger or out of another wrong emotion.*
> *At times I have been blind to the need for compassion. Please give me*
> *sight to see when there is someone along my way who is in need. Help*
> *me to obey Jesus' instructions to go and do likewise. Thank You.*

The Funniest Thing

A funny thing happened to me the first year I went to the Pro Bowl. I was the victim of one of the oldest tricks in the book. After putting on my gear for practice, I start burning and itching in a very embarrassing place. I was hopping around trying to get relief and saying, "Oh, ouch." I thought there was something wrong with me. The other guys had put red-hot in my jock.

I went through the entire practice and never figured out what was wrong. The other players were cracking up. The coach was too. I thought they were just telling jokes, but they were laughing at me.

It didn't dawn on me that I'd been had until a couple of days later when they got someone else, too. I overheard one player exclaim, "Hey man, somebody put red-hot in my jock! Who did that?" I'd been initiated. Welcome to the Pro Bowl.

Football players can be intense; we have to be if we are going to excel. But we also know how to laugh. One time when the Bruce Lee kung fu movies were popular, players started making strange sounds: "Whoah! Whooah! Whaw!" Al Harris was the main one doing it in our locker room. He yelled a lot. Al was 6-foot-6, went about 280 and was acting like a Ninja.

One day during a game, Al was running down field on a kickoff when a little safety got a good angle on him. Bam! Al's helmet and chinstrap went flying off, and he was out cold!

Later, when we were looking at the game film, Al was there, propped up in a chair with a fat lip and a towel on his neck. We watched the play in slow motion. At the moment he was nailed by the safety, we all went, "Whoah! Whooah! Whaw!" The coaches kept running it over and over and over. Every time his head snapped back and his helmet flew off, we went, "Whoah! Whooah! Whaw!" We never laughed so hard.

We were filled with laughter, and we sang for joy. And the other nations said, "What amazing things the LORD has done for them" (Ps. 126:2).

Football is not in the Bible, but baseball, tennis and motorcycle racing are. What? You do not believe me? Look at the first chapter of Genesis. It all happens in the big inning! (Say the previous sentence very fast and you will get it.) People served in Pharaoh's court (though it doesn't say whether Pharaoh had a good backhand).[1] And there was a wicked Triumph (but no Harleys, sorry).[2] OK, to find sports in the Bible you have to take verses out of context, but at least there is humor there.

Puns not your thing? OK, think about Peter. He did some absolutely side-splitting things. I imagine some of his foot-in-mouth comments made Jesus smile, if not chortle.

"Peter, let me wash your feet," Jesus commanded.

"No way, Lord," the disciple retorted.

"If I don't wash your feet, you won't belong to Me."

"Ok then," Peter responded. "How about my head and hands while You're at it!"[3]

Jesus must have shaken His head and rolled His eyes.

What else would make Jesus laugh? Certainly He would not have been amused by anyone's pain or failure. Nor would our Savior have teased or kidded people in a way that might have made them feel bad about themselves. He probably would not have laughed at much of the standup comedy of today, particularly the crude language and antics that advocate violence. But He might have laughed at some of Bill Cosby's clean humor and some of the slapstick of Christian comedians, such as Brandon T. Jackson. More certainly, He shared laughs with His disciples, even though they did not have video to review their funniest stunts like Mike and the Bears did.

It is good to laugh. It is better to laugh like Jesus at whatever would have made Jesus laugh.

Great Creator of Laughter, thank You for the gift of hilarity.
May I use this gift to honor You. I want to laugh at what You think is
funny and be sad about whatever breaks Your heart. Give me
Your mind in these matters. Thank You.

TODAY'S READING: GENESIS 1:24—2:3; 21:5-7; PSALM 126:2;
JOB 8:19-20; LUKE 6:20-26

In the Fog

On December 31, 1988, we beat the Eagles 20-12, but the story of the game occurred in the second quarter. Just before halftime a dense fog rolled off Lake Michigan and onto Soldier Field (where we played our home games). The weather conditions made it an amazing day. I think I enjoyed that game more than any other—ever! I loved it because we played *without coaching.*

When the fog rolled in, we could only see 20 or so yards in any direction. Lack of visibility took away long pass plays, and although the coaches couldn't see much from the sidelines, on the field we could see well enough to keep playing.

The referees told us, "We can see. But the coaches can't see. You feel comfortable with that? You guys want to keep playing?"

"Yeah! We want to play." Both teams enthusiastically agreed.

"Let's play ball!" the refs hollered, and we played.

When I would go over to the sidelines between plays, the coaches would ask, "Did you call what I said?" "What's going on?" They couldn't see a thing.

I told them, "We're winning! That's all I can tell you. We've got 'em."

The game was a miracle. I still get chills thinking about it. Being able to continue playing was an opportunity of a lifetime for me. I loved it because I got to call all of the defensive sets for the entire second half—without any interference from the coaches.

When the fog started coming in, my first thoughts were of the old Charlton Heston version of *The Ten Commandments.* I pictured the scene where the Death Angel passes over those with the marking on their doorposts but killed the firstborn in all the other houses. In the movie, the fog came creeping in from a dry ice machine. In our game it came in from Lake Michigan. In both cases, it was dense.

As he was nearing Damascus on this mission, a brilliant light from heaven suddenly beamed down upon him! He fell to the ground and heard a voice saying to him, "Saul! Saul! Why are you persecuting me?" (Acts 9:3-4).

There is a great Bible story in which Jesus talks to one person while, metaphorically speaking, everyone else is kept on the sidelines, lost in a fog. The encounter occurred between Jesus and Saul on the road to Damascus. Similar to what happened with the Bear coaches who couldn't see what was happening on the field, those walking with Saul could only hear thunder.

Saul was purpose-driven, but initially it was the wrong purpose. Before his encounter in the fog, he dedicated himself to eradicating Christians.[1] Once the fog lifted, he did a 180-degree turn and immersed himself in converting to Christianity as many people as he could.

Jesus chose to use a bright light—brighter than the sun—to blind Saul and a voice of thunder to get his attention. In this situation, Jesus and Paul were the only ones on the field. In the supernatural realm, an intense battle raged. To whom would Saul's soul belong? Whichever way it went, it wouldn't belong to Saul. Yes, the decision was his, but his soul wasn't. Satan had owned it since Saul had become old enough to be responsible for his own actions. God wanted Saul's soul, but Saul had to decide which way he would go.

Some say God knew what it would take to convince Saul, so Saul never really had a choice. But that conclusion doesn't fit with the rest of Scripture. Everyone has a choice. God will get our attention, but He won't violate our free will.

It is true that God doesn't get everyone's attention the way He got Saul's. Nor does Jesus wrestle with everyone the same way that he wrestled with Saul. But the outcome can be the same. When Saul went to the sidelines, the people asked, "What's happening?"

Saul, who became Paul, replied, "Jesus won. That's all you need to know."

Dear Lover of My Soul, the battle is too important to stay on the sidelines in a fog. I want to be in the game. Please put me in. Thank You.

Friends and Quarterbacks

Being a middle linebacker gave me opportunities to see the other team's quarterback up close and personal. I guess that's why people often ask for my opinion as to which quarterbacks were the all-time best.

I have always had the utmost respect for my opponents, especially those who played hard and with class. With this in mind, I rate Joe Montana as the best quarterback. He wasn't the greatest athlete. Steve Young was physically more able, but Montana played hard and with class. He was the best leader, plus he had charisma, remarkable smarts and quickness. He was by far the best at reading and countering a blitz. If we were going to rush Montana, we had to do it correctly—if we didn't, he would beat us.

ESPN picked Johnny Unitas as number two of all-time. I must admit that I did not see Unitas play nearly as much as I saw the others—and he was no doubt great—but in my book, Dan Marino was the second-best quarterback. If a team had to run a long down-field play, and if they had some great receivers, then Marino was the man. He had a stronger arm than Montana and could kill you down field with a 30- or 40-yard pass.

John Elway is my third pick. After that, I do not have a specific order. Roger Staubach's belief in his ability to bring the team back from behind put him a cut above many others. Jim Kelly's rapport with his guys is legendary. Steve Young was probably the best athlete and the best running quarterback. Fran Tarkenton was the best scrambler. Jim McMahon is head and shoulders the craziest quarterback to ever win a Super Bowl, and no quarterback of any era had more grit. Of the young quarterbacks, Michael Vick has the potential to make the grade—we shall see.

That's my list. While I limited my choices to quarterbacks who played in my lifetime—and I only actually played with McMahon—I admire and respect all of the great quarterbacks, and count many of them as friends.

For the sake of my brothers and friends, I will say, "Peace be with you" (Ps. 122:8).

What strikes me about Mike's list is not just his expert analysis but also the friendship factor. He respected his opponents.

As I reflect on Mike's words, my thoughts drift back a million years to when I played basketball at Oregon State. In those days, after the game we often hung out with players from the other team. When I played in the NBA with the Lakers, the same was true.

Times have changed. Nowadays respecting an opponent is not cool. Today's culture almost demands that players hate, bad-mouth and squash the opposition—sometimes teammates, too. "Show no mercy" seems to be the maxim of the day, but it is not new. In fact, it is very old.

In the pre-prophet days, opponents weren't praised—they were humiliated. For example, God wanted the Amalekites eliminated; David bad-mouthed Goliath before he killed him, and when God's people took the Promised Land other tribes and cities quivered in fear.

Thankfully, when Jesus came, everything changed. He said, "You have heard that the Law of Moses says, 'Love your neighbor' and hate your enemy. But I say, love your enemies!"[1] This teaching was the exact opposite of what the Jewish rulers (Pharisees) taught. Some Pharisees actually implied that hatred was God's means of judging an enemy.' Jesus put that kind of thinking to rest. New Testament teaching tells us that even the demons and the devil are not to be scoffed at.[3]

We can apply the same principle of respect to war. Consider the American War of Independence. It occurred between Christian nations that had respect for each other and followed rules of conduct. Today, in the same way, in our just war against terrorism we maintain rules regarding torture and minimizing collateral damage. What God has created is to be respected. Life is precious.

This principle even applies to something as trivial as sports—there is no room for disrespect. If God won't allow it in heaven, we shouldn't take part in it on Earth. We should make friends with our opponents when we can and always show respect for them.

Creator of Heaven and Earth, give me a deep appreciation for Your creation of life. Help me to respect it, fight for it and preserve it. And Lord, as I go through the events of this day, remind me to love my enemies, respect God-ordained authority and look at life and competition through the eyes of Jesus. Help me to make friends out of enemies. Thank You.

TODAY'S READING: 1 SAMUEL 15:4-23; 17:41-49; MATTHEW 5:43-48; LUKE 6:27-38; JUDE 1:8-11; 2 PETER 2:8-11

Shufflin' on Down

I was in junior high when I first started playing football. At first, I talked trash because everyone else did. But I seemed to be the only one getting hurt by it, so I said to myself, *Just be quiet and play the game.*

When I was on the Bears, guys talked a lot of trash. It embarrassed me sometimes. Perhaps the loudest trash we ever talked was in a video called "The Super Bowl Shuffle."

> We are the Bears shufflin' crew. Shufflin' on down, doin' it for you. We're so bad, we know we're good. Blowin' your mind like you knew we would.

We hadn't even been to a Super Bowl yet, and we had just lost a game to Miami. This was trash talk taken to a new level. It was arrogant, which is different from jabbering in the flow of the game.

In a game, if a guy hit me in the back, I might have said, "Hey, is that all you've got? Is that the best you can do with my back turned?" I do remember playing Cleveland on a Monday night. The Browns had a big lineman who tried to take my legs out a couple of times. I yelled at him while he was in the huddle. I said, "When you come to the line, I'm going to whip you like a little boy." When he came to the line I started talking and he rose up and went to the other end of the line. I said, "No, no, no. Don't run. Come back over here. I'm talking to you." We went at it a few times, but only in the flow of the game. There was nothing personally denigrating and I did not use profanity.

I rarely talked trash. I only "educated" people when they were going for my or my teammate's legs. I wanted them to think about what they were doing. But I did it legally—never dirty. There is no place in the game for cheap shots.

> About noontime Elijah began mocking them. "You'll have to shout louder," he scoffed, "for surely he is a god! Perhaps he is deep in thought, or he is relieving himself. Or maybe he is away on a trip, or he is asleep and needs to be wakened!" (1 Kings 18:27).

As a player, Mike Singletary didn't talk much smack. What little trash he used was never obscene and rarely demeaning. Not perfect, but not so bad. It's good to know that Mike mostly maintained his boundaries. Watching what words we use is tough to do—I know firsthand.

Some words are obviously out of bounds, but other chatter is tougher to call. I was in my fifties and still hadn't learned. During a game of hoops, I kept faking the guy guarding me out of his unmentionables. He kept calling a violation. I finally said, "Just because you've never seen the move before doesn't make it illegal." I kept the game honest without getting mad, but I could have been kinder.

The best trash talker in the Bible didn't care about being perfect. In a showdown on Mt. Carmel, Ahab and Jezebel's god—represented by 850 prophets—were pitted against the lone Elijah and his God. The deity that brought down fire would be the winner.

Elijah addressed the onlookers: "How long are you going to waver between two opinions? If the Lord is God, follow him! But if Baal is God, then follow him!"[1]

Elijah wasn't talking trash—yet. The false prophets ranted and raved all morning. Then Elijah went into action.

> About noontime Elijah began mocking them. "You'll have to shout louder," he scoffed, "for surely he is a god! Perhaps he is deep in thought, or he is relieving himself. Or maybe he is away on a trip, or he is asleep and needs to be wakened!"[2]

That was pure trash.

Elijah talked smack until around 2:30 P.M. and then set up the show. At 3:00 P.M. he switched from trash to prayer, "O Lord, answer me! Answer me so these people will know that you, O Lord, are God and that you have brought them back to yourself."[3] God answered with fire and the people cried out, "The Lord is God! The Lord is God!"[4] God blessed Elijah's smack.

What are the guidelines for godly trash talk? Make sure your anger is righteous, don't use profanity and defend the faith.

Almighty Defender, help me to remember to let You defend me, give me the courage to defend the faith, guard me from anger, cursing and obscenities. Remind me to control my tongue for Jesus' sake. Amen.

TODAY'S READING: 1 KINGS 18:20-40; PSALM 5:8-10; ROMANS 3:9-18; JAMES 5:12

The Cost of Compromise

It takes talent to win, but a team cannot concede character for talent. I saw what happens when this kind of compromise comes into the camp.

In 1988, Wilbur Marshall, Otis Wilson, Jim McMahon and Willie Gault were gone. What's more, a bunch of guys were hurt. The Bears's management brought in about 10 fantastic rookies. We had a very young team, and everyone was excited about our prospects.

The rooks were hungry and they wanted to win. They also sought veteran leadership. We grew together as a team and eventually went to the conference championship game, where we lost to San Francisco.

With success, management was thinking, *Wow, we can win with these kids. We don't need high-priced egos. This saves us a lot of money and headaches.* The 1988 batch of rookies was one thing, but having rookies as the foundation of the team was another. The move away from veteran leadership compromised quality and, to a lesser degree, it also compromised character. I saw it coming.

The next group of rookies lacked a work ethic, had no idea of a team concept and didn't really understand the cost of winning. There was no one who was willing to sit with an assistant coach day in and day out to learn the system inside and out. They didn't even know how to dream. It wasn't in them.

With compromise, the Bears changed. For example, in our first regular season game we lost to Tampa Bay. After the game, I realized several guys had quit. They had just given up when the outcome of the game was still in doubt. That was unlike the Bears. We never quit.

One rookie said, "Well, Mike, you win some and you lose some." I didn't say anything to him. If I could have made a difference, I would have. I was in my eleventh year as a Bear.

The team had changed. Management started it. The coaches perpetuated it. And the players demonstrated it. I played one more year. Compromise had come into the camp. It was time to go.

And all the churches will know that I am the one who searches out the thoughts and intentions of every person. And I will give to each of you whatever you deserve (Rev. 2:23).

When compromise comes into a spiritual camp, it will cost the blessing of God. That's what happened to Joshua.

Joshua had never lost a battle—until Ai. The loss was not due to anything Joshua did; rather, compromise had come into his camp and he didn't know it. Achan had coveted some gold and silver obtained from a previously defeated foe. Only one problem: God had banned the booty. Achan took it anyway and hid it in his tent. The compromise cost the camp God's blessing and the men of Ai defeated Joshua's army. That hadn't happened to the Jewish people since they had left Egypt.[1]

Joshua was smart enough to seek God to search out the problem. God led him to Achan, who was judged and removed, and God's blessing returned. In this case, the temptation to compromise came in the form of possessions. But it takes other forms as well. For the Bears it was a loss of character. For Moses it was pride.

Moses compromised when God told him to call water out of a stone.[2] Moses took some of the credit for the miracle. In essence, he told his people, "We are going to provide water for you." It was the plural pronoun "we" that compromised the camp. Until then Moses had always given God all the glory. This time, in his pride, he tried to keep some for himself.

Moses lost his right to lead. The reason was clear: "But the Lord said to Moses and Aaron, 'Because you did not trust me enough to demonstrate my holiness to the people of Israel, you will not lead them into the land I am giving them!'"[3] Moses could only look at the promised land. He wouldn't be allowed to go in.

How about you? Do you have anything hidden in your camp that God has banned? Things like coveting, greed, pride, lust or the like? Root it out before it takes you down. You don't want to miss going into your promised land.

All knowing Father in Heaven, You are aware of my thoughts and motives. I'm sorry for the times I have harbored sin in my mind and life. I don't want to steal the glory from You. Don't give up on me. Guard me against compromise. I want to do Your will. Amen.

TODAY'S READING: JOSHUA 7:1—8:2; NUMBERS 20:6-10; PSALM 139:23-24; REVELATION 2:18-29

Two Kinds of Character

Longtime Bears quarterback Jim McMahon had fiber. He was a character, too. The fiber was good. Every quarterback should have that. But here is a difference between being a character and having character.

Jim was a rare guy. Coach Ditka would be right in his face, calling him all sorts of names. Jim would glance around and say, "Let me have some water." He was totally unaffected.

Jim's unfazed response would make Ditka madder. Jim would cut to the chase, "Hey, look. Is that going to make me any better? I don't think so. What do you want me to do, man? Cut out all this foolishness! What do you want me to do?" The looks, the comments—those two knew how to dance.

We never had to worry about Jim giving his best. He would play no matter how hurt he was and he'd do everything within his power to win. However, his off-the-field pranks were legendary. If I needed someone to whom I could trust my life, I would not necessarily pick Jim. Todd Bell would be my first choice. He was a man of character.

Todd—who in early 2005 died prematurely—was physically the strongest safety I've ever seen, and he covered my back. A lineman running toward us could weigh 280, but Todd could put him flat on his tail. Todd weighed about 215, but he was a missile. He knew how to hit and how to intimidate.

Todd was a Christian who deeply loved the Lord. At times he didn't know how to express himself and was very quiet, but when he stepped onto that football field it was life and death, like it was to me. When he played, he believed he was a great player. We were kindred sprits in that regard. Off the field, we were roommates. When Todd said he was going to do something, he did it. I don't ever remember Todd lying. I don't ever remember Todd swearing—not on or off the field. He was always the same guy. That is the kind of character every player should have.

May integrity and honesty protect me, for I put my hope in you (Ps. 25:21).

Sampson was quite a character, but he had a flaw. He was a man of high calling with amazing God-given strength, but he had a weakness for the ladies.

Raised as a Nazirite, Sampson didn't cut his hair or consume alcohol. He was consecrated by his parents and reared in devotion to God. But like so many young people who go off to college, Sampson put his parents' faith on the shelf and pursued pleasure. Although he didn't drink at frat parties, he slept around. He visited a prostitute in Gaza[1] and had a costly affair with Delilah.[2]

Some think Samson's strength came from his hair. Not so. His power came from the Holy Spirit, which was quenched when the consequences of sin finally caught up with him. Sex blinded Sampson, both spiritually and physically. He was a character with a flaw who fell short of what he could have been.

Like Sampson, John the Baptist was quite a character. Unlike Sampson, John maintained his character right up to the time he lost his head.

John appeared on the scene when he came out of the wilderness dressed as a Neanderthal. The Baptizer was a no-frills, trailer-trash kind of guy. His favorite meal was warm, fresh, honey-dipped locusts. Disheveled and dirty, he wore a cheap cloth made of camel hair.

John came with the assignment to announce the coming of a King. I would have expected God to go with someone like Ed McMahon. Ed introduced Johnny Carson for more than 30 years. But no, instead of a smooth talker, God went with coarse camel hair and leather.

But John was so good at introducing the Messiah that Jesus said he was the greatest man ever born.[3] John was a character who never compromised his character.

What kind of character are you?

Dear God, forgive me for compromising my character.
Don't allow me to become content with sin. I choose to repent of
my past. I want to be a person of character. Thank You.

TODAY'S READING: JUDGES 15:14—16:31; JOHN 11:7-19;
EPHESIANS 3:16-19; JAMES 1:2-4

The Fridge

The Fridge could have been great—*scary great*. Instead, he was just a phenomenon. What he was and what he could have become are night and day.

William "The Refrigerator" Perry was almost 6-foot-2 and weighed 320 pounds. From a flat-footed position, he could jump and dunk a basketball with two hands. The man could move, run and leap. He was incredibly quick.

The Fridge played for the Bears and could throw a football almost the length of the field. He would surprise us by effortlessly hopping up on a chair with both feet. He had huge shoulders and long powerful arms. He was a unique combination of abilities, a natural athlete—but he had a tough time disciplining himself—a very tough time. Buddy Ryan saw William's talent, but also saw the lack of self-discipline and respect for the game. If the Fridge had only improved his self-discipline, the sky would have been the limit as to how great he could have been. He would have been a mauler. It wouldn't have been fair to the other teams to let him play. He might have become the first illegal player. As undisciplined as he was, he was still amazing.

One Monday night, Coach Ditka gave him the football during a game and it was the beginning of the end. The success and attention went straight to his head. He couldn't move without bumping into a television camera. Everybody wanted to interview The Fridge. And he made millions of dollars in endorsements. How could it not go to his head? It was probably more than any one of us could handle.

The Fridge was not a good listener and didn't receive advice very well. Most of the time he spoke as if he had all of the answers. His favorite response was, "Uh, I uh, uh, I know that. I know that."

Just as my junior high school coach had encouraged me, I encouraged William: "Fridge, if you would just take some voice lessons it would help you a lot."

The Fridge responded, "Uh, I uh, uh, I know that. I'm gonna do that. OK, OK."

The Fridge was an amazing phenomenon. But, he could have become so much more!

If you need wisdom—if you want to know what God wants you to do—ask him, and he will gladly tell you. (Jas. 1:5).

Just as The Fridge failed to become as great as he might have become, many Christians fail to become all that God intends them to be. Why? Because of what I call éclairs in the refrigerator.

Let me explain: Assume you're dieting, but one day you walk by a bakery. You are hungry, so you go in and buy two chocolate éclairs. Upon arriving home you feel guilty, so you put the uneaten éclairs in the refrigerator. You go into the living room, kneel and pray, "Oh God, help me to not eat those chocolate éclairs!"

How much power is in that prayer? The answer is to be found in the analysis of your heart. Why did you put the éclairs in the refrigerator? To save them, of course! You wanted to make sure that the pastries wouldn't spoil before you reached a point when you could justify eating them. In other words, you had already made up your mind to live against your prayers.

You prayed and asked God to help keep you from eating the chocolate éclairs, but you were really waiting for the right opportunity to chow down. Perhaps you were hoping God would say, "Oh, go ahead and eat stuff that is bad for you." You were giving lip service to God or trying to manipulate Him. Either way, you were double-minded.

Double-minded prayers say one thing but mean another, or ask one thing but hope for a different answer. You can't get away with that when you're dealing with God. How can there be power in a prayer when you really aren't open to His answer? The result of such praying is obvious—there is no power!

Just as James 1:5-8 explains the problem, it also provides the solution: "Draw close to God, and God will draw close to you. Wash your hands, you sinners; purify your hearts, you hypocrites."[1] Stop saying, "Uh, I uh uh, I know that. I'm gonna do that. OK. OK." Stop sinning. Get the éclairs out of your refrigerator and do what God wants you to do.

Dear Forgiving Father, I'm tired of my will not matching Your
will. I'm tired of being double-minded and harboring sin in my heart.
I'm tired of continuing to come to You concerning my reoccurring sin,
but I will keep coming until I get it right. Lord Jesus, help me to
get the éclairs out of my mind and heart. Amen.

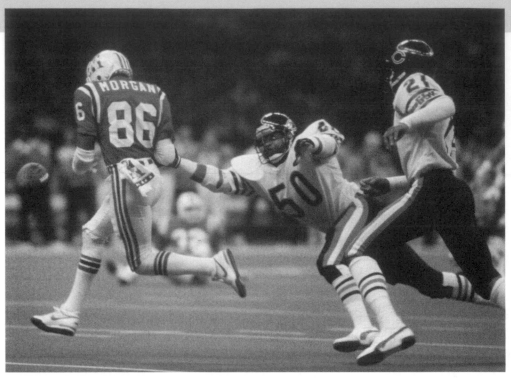

Just super. In Super Bowl XX, Mike Singletary causes Patriots' receiver Stanley Morgan to lose the football (above). Chicago's linebackers (below) were lauded for stopping Steve Grogan and the Patriot offense.

Farewell. In December 1992, Mike ran onto Soldier Field for the last time (below). He was honored for his Hall of Fame career (above) and said a few words to his fans (right).

Buckle Up

Most NFL players were bigger than me. I got used to going up against them and found ways to take advantage of my size. I had quick feet, so it was hard for larger guys to get a bead on me. I also delivered a solid blow, and as a result, not too many guys wanted to tangle for long. However, there were two exceptions: John Hannah and Dan Dierdorf.

I first faced Hannah during a game in New England. As the Patriots lined up for their first offensive play, I heard grunting, growling and snarling. I looked to my right and saw a blood-red face squeezed under the edges of a helmet. It rested on top of a massive body that was supported by huge pillar-like legs. This man was built like a Mack truck. With the snap of the football, he barreled toward me and we collided. He didn't flinch—not on that play, not ever. That was John Hannah.

Dan Dierdorf was another tough foe. He was at the end of his career when I came into the league, and he had moved from tackle over to center for St. Louis. Although I had studied game film and I knew his tendencies, the first time we played against the Cardinals, no one had pointed him out to me.

I will never forget our first collision. Bam! Most hits are pretty much the same but Dierdorf loosened my helmet. I collected myself and thought, *Who the heck is that?* We collided a few more times. I thought, *I'd better buckle up my stuff here and get ready for this guy.*

The next play—bam! *Whew*! I thought, *Better buckle up a little more*. It wasn't long before I was looking for some more buckles. We tore it up the whole game. Dierdorf was bringing it—and he was on his last leg. I wondered what he had been like in his prime. He must have been something special.

John Hanna and Dan Dierdorf were gridiron goliaths.

And the ones who win this battle against the world are the ones who believe that Jesus is the Son of God (1 John 5:5).

The man across the line probably outweighed the boy by more than 300 pounds. The Bible describes this hulk:

> A giant nearly ten feet tall stepped out from the Philistine line into the open, Goliath from Gath. He had a bronze helmet on his head and was dressed in armor—126 pounds of it! He wore bronze shin guards and carried a bronze sword. His spear was like a fence rail—the spear tip alone weighed over fifteen pounds. His shield bearer walked ahead of him.[1]

This giant of a man taunted the forces of Israel, and all of God's people were filled with fear—all except one. David was filled with righteous indignation. Goliath's antics simply ticked him off.[2]

The Jewish people were paralyzed when they realized that they could not muster up the brute force it would take to knock out Goliath. Only David understood the spiritual significance of the encounter. In the eyes of most of the people, Goliath appeared to be too big to hit. But David knew that with God, Goliath was too big to miss. The Goon from Gath could snort, snarl, yell and talk trash all he wanted. David wasn't intimidated.

David knew God well enough to be confident. In fact, David was so sure that he would win that he buckled up and ran toward Goliath. David was eager to get it on. The boy wanted to get something into that giant's thick skull, and it wasn't an idea or a thought. It was a rock. And he did. Thus, David defeated the enemy of the Jewish people.

Who or what are your Goliaths? Perhaps it's your boss or your in-laws. Maybe it's financial difficulty or depression. Is the thought of leading a purposeless life filling you with fear? Take a stand. Grab your Bible, buckle up and use verses as stones. With the Word, any Goliath can fall. With God, we win.

Great God of Victory, sometimes my Goliaths appear too big and I get scared. Show me that with You no problem is too large. Give me the faith to run into battle with You at my side. Thank You.

TODAY'S READING: 1 SAMUEL 17:1-58; ROMANS 13:11-14; 2 CORINTHIANS 10:1-5; EPHESIANS 6:10-20

 Glorious

I've had many special moments playing football, but two stand out as being absolutely glorious.

In a game against Minnesota, I tried a new technique using my hands. It worked well until I hit this one guy. My hand got caught between our helmets and I squished off the end of one of my fingers.

I went upstairs and the doctor poured peroxide on it, sewed it back on, bandaged it and said, "You're watching the rest of the game."

"I didn't come here to watch the game," I retorted. "I'm playing!"

"You can't. You could mess up your hand," he cautioned.

The doctor's attempts to reason with me didn't work. I got back to the sidelines late in the fourth quarter, just as we fumbled the ball inside our five-yard line. If the Vikings scored, the game would be over; they would win. As I went back into the game I walked to the Minnesota huddle and yelled, "You will not score."

They screamed, "Get out of our huddle!"

I said, "I'm just telling you, you will not score. . . . I'll bet you don't score and we'll win."

One Viking said, "You're on."

That verbal exchange fired up our defense and we stopped them four downs in a row. They did not score and we did win. For me, it was a glorious moment. I've never been any higher.

That was the only time I ever went into the other team's huddle. It was cocky. However, several weeks later I got a gold quarter in the mail. One Viking showed a lot of class.

The other glorious moment came during a game against the Rams. Toward the end of the fourth quarter, the Rams' Eric Dickerson fumbled. My teammate Wilbur Marshall picked up the football and ran for a touchdown. As he entered the end zone it began to snow, but the sun was also peaking between some clouds. The glistening on his back was magic.

My career could have ended on either of those events. Both were a rush! Both were glorious.

Father, I want these whom you've given me to be with me, so they can see my glory. You gave me the glory because you loved me even before the world began! (John 17:24).

The word "glorious" means "beautiful in a way that inspires wonder or joy."[1] Mike's moments were glorious for Bears' fans, but I'm sure that their opponents missed seeing the magic. God's glory works much the same way.

God's glory is obvious to people when they look for it. Consider Moses. After seeing God on a mountaintop, Moses returned to the Israelites in the valley below. Almost everyone in the crowd knew exactly why Moses' face was aglow. But there were a few who said, "Send him to a dermatologist, he needs some Oxy 10." The doubters missed seeing God's glory.[2]

Every morning for 40 years, this same group of Israelites had food appear in the form of manna. But some of the people thought the heavenly food wouldn't be there the next morning, so they collected more than a day's worth. They got worms and missed seeing God's glory.[3]

Moses and these same Israelites were guided by a pillar of cloud during the day and a pillar of fire at night. The pillars were evidence of God's Glory, but some of the Israelites wondered why it was always foggy. Others complained, "We're too old for a night light." The whiners missed seeing God at work.[4]

In the same way, many people miss seeing God's glory in Christ. Thirty-five passages record His miracles. He did 17 healings, sometimes mending more than one person at a time. He also performed six demonic deliverances, raised three people from the dead, orchestrated two supernatural fish catches and oversaw two major feedings. He turned water to wine, stilled a storm, strolled on the water, placed bucks in a bass and shriveled a fig tree. There are 12 references to other miracles and the New Testament authors indicate that they only recorded a small percentage of what Christ did.

Jesus used a word, a touch and a little spit to work wonders. I've seen moms do some amazing things with spit rubbed on kid's faces, but no mom ever made a blind man see. How obvious can God's glory be?

Glorious Lord, thank You for the endless demonstrations of Your glory. Give me eyes to see and ears to hear. I don't want to miss anything. And thank You for Your Son, Jesus Christ, in whose name I pray. Amen.

TODAY'S READING: EXODUS 13:17-21; 16:13-31; 34:29-34;
JOHN 17:22-24; 2 PETER 1:12-18

The Perfect Play

One primary duty of a linebacker is to hit opposing players. We work on timing, angles, leverage, point of impact and a zillion other aspects of the perfect hit. In my 12 years with the Bears, I delivered some great hits.

It would be impossible to pick a favorite, but the time I hit Joe Delaney in a game against the Kansas City Chiefs would be at or near the top of my list. Joe started running into the hole and I met him with every ounce of strength I had. It was a great pop, a solid collision—orchestrated to perfection. After the hit, Joe had to leave the game. It was within the rules, so I didn't have to apologize. In fact, Joe understood. He's a football player.

My most important hit came against Eric Dickerson. When defending against a great running back like Eric, if I blinked, he'd be gone. So I had to stay focused and make sure that I had the right angle on him. Eric was a big guy, tough and a great competitor. He wasn't afraid of anybody. I enjoyed playing against him.

It was third-and-one. If Eric's team got the first down, they would be in position to kick a field goal. If they fell short, then they would have to punt. We couldn't let them score even three points because the winner of the game would go to the Super Bowl.

Eric and I came into the hole at the same time. I stood him up for no gain. They had to punt. We actually held Eric to 23 total yards that game, but that particular stop was huge—it was perfect. It might have been the play that put us in the big game. It certainly put us one step closer.

For God so loved the world that he gave his only Son, so that everyone who believes in him will not perish but have eternal life (John 3:16).

The Old Testament records some of Israel's greatest plays. God—who is the Ultimate Coach—designed them, so they were perfect.

What happened at Jericho was genius. The city was impregnable. So God had His people sing and worship Him while taking seven laps around the exterior. Then, bam—a trumpet blast brought the walls down.[1] No field goal, and no Super Bowl for the people of Jericho.

Another time, Gideon ran a trick play that would have made him a Pro Bowler. He scared his foes by banging pots, shouting and lighting up the night. As a result, he didn't have to kill them—they killed themselves.[2]

Jael pulled a fast one on Sisera. She lured the enemy warrior into her tent and, while he slept, killed him by driving a tent peg through his temple. That was a big hit for Barak and the ten thousand warriors from the Jewish tribes of Naphtali and Zebulun.[3]

What we call Passover wins my vote for the greatest Old Testament play. God stuck it to Pharaoh and killed every firstborn child of every family that had not applied sacrificial blood to the doorway of their houses. The firstborn of each of the household animals died as well. God, however, had warned the Jewish people and He passed over their homes. Pharaoh had finally had enough and decided to let God's people go.[4]

God's all-time best play came on the cross. Mel Gibson's *The Passion of the Christ* was a magnificent portrayal of what happened on Calvary. This singular "play" (I use this word in the context of this reading, but it was obviously much more than a play) surpasses all other plays in human history. Jesus' death and resurrection solved our problem of sin.[5] Because He stood in the gap for us, we no longer need to be separated from God. Neither do we need to take the brunt of Satan's hits. In fact, Jesus' perfect hit not only opened the way for us to be restored to God, but it also was the blow that put our enemy out of the game.

Marvelous Author of History, thank You for the truth of the past
that allows me to see You in action. Thank You for providing enough
truth that my faith need not be blind. Thank You for these glimpses of You
for the times when I drift away and make You seem distant.
And thank You for always drawing me back. Thank You.

TODAY'S READING: EXODUS 12:21-36; JOSHUA 6:1-21;
JUDGES 4:12-22; 7:19-23; JOHN 19:28-30

When I was a kid, my siblings and I would play Simon Says. I liked being Simon. So much fun!

The object of the game, of course, was to do what Simon said *only* when the words "Simon says" preceded the instructions. "Simon says, 'Jump on one foot'" meant that everyone had to jump on one foot. If Simon only said, "Jump on one foot," but didn't precede it with "Simon says," no one was supposed to move. Anyone who did was eliminated.

In a way, the Simon Says game happens on the gridiron. Simon wants to trick people into jumping at the wrong time; one team's offense wants to sucker the other team's defense into defending the wrong play.

This works when an offense establishes a running game. On play after play, the quarterback will hand the ball off to a running back. The setup for every play looks the same and the defense jumps to stop the run. After a series of running plays, the quarterback will set up his offense to look like another run. At the last second, instead of handing off, the quarterback throws a pass. If the defense is not alert, it might be caught defending the wrong play. Having too many players rushing the quarterback would leave a downfield receiver wide open.

In Simon Says, players have to listen closely to Simon's words or they might get caught jumping at the wrong time. In football, defensive players have to watch closely for signs that tip off a change in an offensive play. This is called "reading the keys." When football players key, they recognize or read a quarterback's habit of licking his fingers before he throws a pass, a lineman's putting his hand down in a different way or an opponent's showing anticipation on his face.

Once in Minnesota, Vikings' quarterback Wade Wilson's expression gave him away. He set up for a run, but there was no Simon Says. I knew that meant pass. When Wade hit the pocket, I was there to tackle him before he could throw the ball. After the game he said, "You got me good."

This time Jonah obeyed the LORD's command and went to Nineveh (Jonah 3:3).

Jonah probably would not have been very good at playing Simon Says. He would have jumped at the wrong time or stood on one foot when he was supposed to touch his nose.

How do I know?

Well, look at how Jonah failed to key in on God's words. God dispatched the prophet to Nineveh. God even preceded His instructions with a "God says." How did Jonah respond? Instead of booking a flight to Nineveh, he bought a one-way ticket on a boat sailing in the opposite direction.[1]

The most famous parts of Jonah's tale come next. While at sea, the prophet's vessel was struck by a huge storm. Jonah did read that key from God, but it was obvious. It would have been like Wade Wilson yelling his next play to Mike Singletary before the ball was snapped.

Jonah pled before God to spare the ship, but it sounded more like someone asking to stay in the game even after he or she had jumped when there was no "Simon says." The sailors in Jonah's boat would have none of that. They tossed the prophet into the sea where he was swallowed by a whale.[2]

God was kinder than Simon. Despite Jonah's antics, God said the prophet could stay in the game, so to speak. Preceded by another "God says," the Lord showed mercy and again dispatched Jonah to Nineveh.[3]

As God had instructed, Jonah finally warned the townspeople that their wicked city was about to be destroyed. The people of Nineveh repented and asked God to spare them.[4] He did, which made Jonah mad. If the prophet had been reading God's keys, he might have foreseen the next move. God had set Nineveh up for the nuclear option, but changed to mercy.[5] He had even signaled the change with the way He showed mercy toward Jonah.

Of course, this is not a perfect illustration, because Jonah and God are on the same side. Nonetheless, it shows how we need to go to Nineveh when God says, "Go"; but before blowing up the place, we need to know what God really wants.

Great God of Mercy, You do not want me to be unaware of what You are doing and what You are going to do. Give me spiritual eyes to see and a supernatural ability to understand. I want to be alert to reading the keys to what You have planned. Thank You.

Samurai

Doug Plank was a strong safety, and he is the one who first called me Samurai.

If Doug had been a couple inches taller, he would have made a tremendous inside linebacker. He was ferocious and could knock a person out. Actually Doug was the guy who taught me to make sure that I made clean tackles. If I didn't complete the job, he would be there to help make sure that an opposing runner did not gain any extra yards. And I didn't want his help because that would imply that I could not do the job myself. In fact, I worked overtime on my tackling skills specifically because I didn't want Doug showing me up.

Doug hit really hard. He could pulverize a person. And he was always willing to make certain the other guy was down.

This is an aside, but it was rather funny to watch. Doug was so intense that during practice Coach Ditka sometimes would say, "Doug! Let me tell you, we're not hitting today in practice. I don't want you to hit anybody."

Doug would say, "Yes, Sir. Yes, Sir. Yes, Sir!"

Doug liked to speak in threes.

With the first pass in practice, Doug would forget what Coach had said and would nuke the receiver.

"I'm sorry, Coach. I'm sorry. I'm sorry."

Plank was a fantastic player and fun to watch, both in a game and at practice. What a great guy! I am glad that he is the one who tagged me with my nickname.

Over the years people have called me many things. I didn't like Tasmanian Devil. The devil part never agreed with me. I didn't like Chainsaw either. That had negative connotations connected to horror movies. Samurai seemed to fit better.

I could get pretty animated on the field, waving my arms around a lot. It reminded Doug of the classic John Belushi *Saturday Night Live* Samurai routine.

Buddy Ryan had lots of nicknames for me, but sometimes he called me Samurai, too.

He immediately led him to Jesus. Jesus took one look up and said, "You're John's son, Simon? From now on your name is Cephas" (or Peter, which means "Rock") (John 1:42, *THE MESSAGE*).

Nicknames can be descriptive. Mike was Samurai because he waved his arms like Belushi. When I played basketball I was Golden Wheels. Gold was rare and wheels were legs—I had the rarest legs anybody had ever seen. I was so slow it looked like I was treading wood.

Sometimes nicknames are terms of endearment, like the ones given to three of Jesus' closest friends. We know Simon better by his nicknames. "Simon," or "Simeon" in Greek, is used to refer to Peter almost 50 times in the Gospels and Acts. The apostle Paul preferred to call Peter "Cephas" and did so eight times. Jesus called Peter "Cephas" once and "Peter" after that. The fisherman is referred to as Peter 148 times.[1] Both "Cephas" and "Peter" mean "rock." In other words, Peter was the first Rocky. Think of a bigger and uglier Sylvester Stallone.

James and John also had nicknames. Jesus called them Boanerges, which can be interpreted to mean the "Sons of Thunder."[2] They might have been known for their booming voices, commanding presence or zealous enthusiasm, but more than likely it was for their tempers that earned them their nicknames. The literal translation of "Boanerges" is "sons of tempest."[3] We see James and John flare up when a Samaritan village turned Jesus away—the brothers asked if they could call down fire to consume the village.[4] John was also known as the beloved disciple and the disciple whom Jesus loved a lot.

God is perfect and doesn't play favorites. Nonetheless, only Peter, James and John were taken to witness the transfiguration, where they saw Jesus talking to Moses and Elijah,[5] and Peter, James and John were the only ones with nicknames. Jesus may not have been playing favorites, but He clearly set them apart from the other disciples.

I'd love it if Jesus had a nickname for me. When I see Him it would be fun to hear, "Welcome, Golden Wheels. You were a piece of work, but you did well with what you had to work with. Enter into My rest."

Would you like Jesus to give you a nickname? What would it be?

Dear Lover of my Soul, it's not that I wouldn't love to sit next to You at a banquet table, because I would, but I don't expect it. Being at the table will be enough. Still, to be known intimately by You would be the thrill of my eternal life. I long to be welcomed by You, to hear my nickname and the words "Well done!" Thank You for the anticipation of it all.

TODAY'S READING: MARK 3:13-19; 9:2-9; 17:1-9; 25:14-30;
LUKE 9:28-36; 51-56, JOHN 1:35-42

Destiny

It is ironic that I am now a coach with the San Francisco 49ers. When I was a player, my worst road trip was to the City by the Bay. To make things worse, the game on that 1991 trip was played on Monday night.

The game itself meant little. We had already secured a play-off berth—all that remained in doubt was whether we would have a home-field advantage in the post-season.

Our first mistake was counting on another team to control our destiny. We figured that on Sunday—the day before our game—the Buffalo Bills would rip the Detroit Lions. As long as Buffalo won, we had home-field advantage in the playoffs and the outcome of our game with the 49ers was moot. We went to San Francisco thinking that we would play our second stringers, thus giving our dinged-up players some time to rest.

Buffalo must have read our game plan. They didn't start their first stringers and lost to the Lions, 17-14 in overtime. The Bills laid an egg. We were on the plane headed to the West Coast when we heard about the game and realized that we had to beat the 49ers on Monday night.

It was too late to change our plans. Like Buffalo, we had prepared to use the second stringers. We were totally embarrassed and lost to San Francisco, 41-0.

Our troubles did not end when the game was over. When we arrived at the airport, we couldn't get a flight home. O'Hare International, in Chicago, was closed due to snow. It was late, so getting a hotel room was not an option—instead, we tried to sleep in the airport. Forty-Niner fans recognized us and ragged on us all night. It was a nightmare. I felt like I had just done something very bad and wanted to take a shower to wash it off, but there was no shower.

That was the worst road trip ever. And it started when we let someone else control our destiny.

I am the way, the truth, and the life. No one can come to the Father except through me (John 14:6).

When I think of destiny, I often contemplate this life and the plan God has for each of us. That is correct thinking. God does have a plan for our lives, but He doesn't make us follow the plan.

Some people correlate destiny with fate, as if there is a cosmic presence or power that makes our individual decisions of no consequence. That is incorrect thinking. God gives us free will. We can let others control our destiny, opt to go our own way or follow His lead. God allows our choice to trump fate almost every time. Whether we choose someone else's way, our own plan or God's best, the choosing is ours. God may influence our thinking, but when it comes to our lives, He rarely does the actual deciding.[1] It's the same when it comes to choosing our eternal destiny.

The Bears put their postseason fate in the hands of someone else. Sometimes we do this with our post-earthly-life fate. We turn to religious leaders or allow someone who doesn't have our best interests in mind to do the deciding for us. That is wrong thinking. Are there any religious leaders or any others who have never made a mistake? None! Well, I don't want the destiny of my soul in the hands of a known mistake maker.

In football, a team wants to decide its own fate. This is where the Bears-Bills-49ers analogy is not a perfect fit when it comes to souls, but we can still learn a lesson. Controlling our own destiny leads to thinking that we win our way to heaven by being a good person, and that too is wrong thinking. We have all made mistakes, even when we had good intentions.

If we cannot entrust our souls to others or ourselves, whom can we trust? Jesus Christ. All but Jesus have made mistakes and have come short of God's plans.[2] If we put our destiny in the hands of anyone other than Christ, we will lose the game of life and it will cost us far more than home-field advantage.

Faithful Father of My Destiny, when it comes to my life
I don't want good or better, I want Your best. And Lord, regarding
eternity, I desire to spend it with You. So, I choose to trust Your Son,
Jesus Christ, with the care and keeping of my soul. Thank You
for Your faithfulness in showing me this truth.

TODAY'S READING: PSALM 42:1-4; PROVERBS 3:5-6; JOHN 14:6-11;
ROMANS 3:21-26; 2 CORINTHIANS 5:21

Wired

If a defense is going to succeed, it needs an engine. I use a car analogy. A vehicle can be beautiful, but if it doesn't have a source of energy, it's not going to run. The rear bumper, steering wheel and turn signals can all be in place, but if there's no engine the car is not going anywhere.

In football, the middle linebacker is the engine of the defense. That was my position. The fuel that runs a defensive engine is leadership, communication and recognition of an opponent's offensive scheme. No wonder I loved being a middle linebacker!

Through the years, some people urged me to try another position. Some coaches thought I would be great at blocking for the ball carrier or at actually carrying the ball. In retrospect, I wish that I had spent some time playing in the offensive backfield—not because I wanted to score touchdowns, but because it would have made me a better linebacker.

Why didn't I? In my mind, being a linebacker and a fullback at the same time created a paradox. As a linebacker, my job was to hit an opponent, attack anyone who had the football and stop offensive plays. The guy with the ball was the enemy. How could I have switched gears and run with the ball?

However, playing fullback would have enhanced my ball handling skills, which was one of my weaknesses. I was taught that linebackers knock people out, so I didn't focus on ball handling skills until I learned the value an interception had in changing the momentum of a game. I usually had good hands during practice; but when the game was on, I was so hyped up that when the ball came my direction, I could not always hold on to it. My hands were too hard.

In games, I deflected many passes and had some interceptions, but I could have been better if I had learned to soften my hands. Playing fullback could have helped me fine-tune my ball handling skills, but I would not have wanted to be a full-time fullback. I was a middle linebacker. I was an engine.

Let's just go ahead and be what we were made to be, without enviously or pridefully comparing ourselves with each other, or trying to be something we aren't (Rom. 12:6, *THE MESSAGE*).

Each of us has what I call a talent mix. This is a set of God-given natural abilities and spiritual gifts. Mike Singletary knew right away that he was wired to be a linebacker. He was an exception. Most people spend years searching for their strengths. Take my daughter Kim as an example.

As a youth, Kim studied dance and took violin lessons. The training was a trial balloon sent up to see if she was the next Isadora Duncan or Itzhak Perlman. When it was clear that she was neither, she moved on. It was not until she was 40 that she discovered that she could sing.

Today, Kim belongs to her church's choir and performs in her community's theater company. She is really good, but she could have been better. If she had known earlier how she was wired, she could have concentrated on singing. As parents, Mary and I missed helping Kim uncover this strength. Had we discovered it sooner, her dance and violin studies could have augmented her vocal talent the same way playing fullback would have helped Mike fine-tune his linebacker skills.

Mike and Kim discovered their talent mixes and went about using what God had given each of them. Some of us, however, find that we are not wired exactly the way we aspired to be wired. A singer may want to be the next American Idol, but God plans to place her on a church's worship team and to be salt in a community theater. A football player may want to be a tight end even though he has Mike's hands.

The apostle Paul addressed this problem of aspiring to the wrong wiring.[1] He instructs us to see the bigger picture. One vocalist may have a great voice, but where would she be without the violin or other instruments? One linebacker may spark a lot of energy on defense, but where would he be without his linemen?

It is when we find our niche that we become most useful in the Kingdom. The younger we are when this happens, the more years God has to maximize our talents and gifts.

Great Giver of Gifts, Talents and Ministries, show me my place in the Body of Christ. I promise to You the best I have to offer. Thank You.

TODAY'S READING: ROMANS 12:3-8; 1 CORINTHIANS 12:4-31

It has been said before, but I have found it to be true: It can be lonely at the top. Let me explain.

At each level of football, I found myself getting after teammates who were slacking or those who were trying, but could try harder. I attempted to be an extension of the coach on the field, and I quarterbacked the defense. Doing these things can alienate you from the other players.

After retiring from the Bears, I went back to some of my former teammates and asked, "How was it having me as the captain? What kind of leader was I?"

My high school teammates said, "We knew that we couldn't let you down. We just knew that you were going to give everything you had, so we had to, too."

My college buddies said, "We really didn't like you because we felt like you were Coach's favorite. You could do no wrong. At the same time, we loved you because we knew that no matter what happened, you were going to stand up for everybody."

My professional teammates said, "Mike, you were crazy intense and extremely demanding, but you didn't ask anything from us that you didn't give yourself."

The exercise was a little scary, but it confirmed some things I have long thought. I knew that I stood alone at every level of competition. I was dedicated to the game and I was intense when I played. Few players could match my mark, so I was set apart. Add to that the facts that I didn't drink, chase women or go wild after games, and it was clear that I was different. There were times when I was lonely.

It would have been nice if I had been one of the guys, but that was not my way. I didn't know how to play any other way. Maybe if I'd had more talent I could have relaxed a bit, but I didn't. I was the guy who came from the ghetto, who was too small and who was dedicated to his family. I was the guy who had reached high society, but really shouldn't have been there.

Yes, sometimes it is lonely at the top.

So you should consider yourselves dead to sin and able to live for the glory of God through Christ Jesus (Rom. 6:11).

Often, people who accomplish great feats are single-minded and lonely. Let me explain.

The most successful among us have others around them and receive lots of attention, but their feats are often done alone. Picture a bird that soars high in the sky, above the flocks of other birds. In the kingdom of winged creatures, there are eagles, falcons and hawks. None of them fly in flocks. Some are bigger than others, but each flies alone. God designs the bird. He chooses the size and species, but how high an individual bird flies is up to the bird.

In the world of conservative Christianity, James Dobson, Billy Graham, T. D. Jakes, Tim LaHaye, Joyce Meyer and Rick Warren are some of the eagles. Each has been used greatly by the Lord. There are lesser-known Christian leaders who represent falcons or hawks. Each person does what God has called him or her to do within his or her sphere of influence.

In Christianity, the great birds of prey are more likely to be birds who pray. The big things that are done for God often are done when God uses an individual in an extraordinary way. Birds who try to do great things without praying will never be great. And those who try to be great for the sake of being great will never be great in the eyes of God. Greatness comes from praying and letting God do the work.

Any bird can be a bird of pray. Prayer makes a sparrow soar like an eagle. Any crow can be a falcon. Any chicken can be a hawk. And even old buzzards, like me, can soar. Prayer miraculously makes the transformation take place. Just remember, the higher a bird flies, the lonelier it gets. Pretty soon it's just the bird and God.

Do you want to be just one of the birds in the flock, or do you want to soar?

Dear Lord of the Heavens and the Sky, I want to soar with You. I am content with how You made me and I will be content with whatever sphere of influence You give me. I don't want anything to keep me from flying as high as I can fly. May You receive the glory for my flight. Amen.

TODAY'S READING: ROMANS 6:5-11; 12:3-8; 1 CORINTHIANS 8:6-7; 12:4-11; 2 CORINTHIANS 5:20-6:10

The Art of Fumbles

Most fumbles are accidental, but a defense should be intentional about causing them. When a defense forces an opponent to make a mistake, it's big. It's great to stop a run, but it's best to actually get the ball.

Players need to be thinking about ways they can cause fumbles. They need to remember to put their face on the football. When they're tackling an opponent, their eyes should go to the football and then they should put their helmet on it.

When it comes to the quarterback, most rushers are so interested in getting a sack that they forget to take a shot at the ball. The more shots a player takes, the more times he can hit the target. The more intentional he gets about creating fumbles, the more fumbles he will cause. Of course, after the ball is dropped, he needs to pounce on it.

When the defense takes the ball away from the offense by a fumble or an interception it's called a turnover, and turnovers are the name of the game. With evenly matched teams, the squad that causes the most turnovers almost always wins.

But just as there are tricks to causing fumbles, there are ways to fall on them. A defender needs to be relaxed and have a sense of urgency at the same time. He needs to realize that he isn't the only one who is going after the bouncing ball.

The trick is for the defender to grab the ball as he falls, pull it to his stomach, wrap his arms around it, pull up his knees and become almost like a turtle. He needs to drop his body on the ground, grab the ball and get into a fetal position. Falling on a football is an art form.

In a full-on dog pile, the ball may change hands several times before the referee digs through the stack of players; so, often the person with the strongest hands wins. Sometimes guys fight at the bottom of the pile, spitting in faces and gouging eyes. It can get a bit nasty, but it is an art.

Live wisely among those who are not Christians, and make the most of every opportunity. Let your conversation be gracious and effective so that you will have the right answer for everyone (Col. 4:5-6).

There are two parts to a turnover. The first part is causing a fumble; the second is falling on it. Occasionally, one person completes both ends, but not often. I cause fumbles. My wife, Mary, falls on them.

Before I lost a vocal cord, I was a traveling preacher. I led workshops on basic training for spiritual warfare and evangelism and spoke at churches. My job was to cause fumbles. I wanted to knock people out of the clutches of the enemy. If the opposition had Christians bound in the arms of sin, I wanted to jar them loose. And for those who didn't understand what Jesus had done for them, I tried to jar them loose with the helmet of salvation. Since losing my voice, my role has changed. I find myself on the sidelines coaching. But in reality, I'm causing more fumbles than ever before by writing.

On the other hand, my wife specializes in falling on fumbles. She is a counselor at the Santa Barbara Rescue Mission. I call what she does "mining for gold." She has to sift through a lot of slag, dirt and mud to find a nugget. It can get nasty; but when she succeeds, it makes the effort worthwhile. Each person who walks through the mission doors has hit bottom. Each one is bouncing around waiting for someone to curl up around him or her and hold him or her tight. Each one is a fumble ready to be pounced on.

On Paul's missionary journeys, his job was to cause fumbles. Depending on the trip, Barnabus, or Silas, and his entourage fell on them. After fixing problem people, these Early Church missionaries then trained the recovered how to both cause and fall on fumbles.

One of the roles of the Church is as a training center where players are taught how to cause and fall on fumbles, and it is a place to bring those who have been recovered, so that they in turn can go out and cause and fall on some more fumbles.

Are you in the game? Are you causing fumbles or falling on them?

Wonderful God of Recovery, please equip me and give me a passion to both cause and fall on fumbles. I want to specialize in turnovers. Show me how and give me a new zeal for this part of Your game plan. Thank You.

TODAY'S READING: ACTS 17:1-9; COLOSSIANS 4:2-6; 1 PETER 3:13-22

Cracking Helmets

I have read a bit about the martial arts. The late Bruce Lee focused on the hand. If he had an open palm, and if he was going to strike a person, the energy and the power would be spread out. The effect would sting, but it wouldn't have the power to knock out an opponent. On the other hand, if he formed a fist, he had focused the energy. If he positioned his body correctly and used his speed, he had the power to knock someone out.

In football, most tackles don't involve a blow. To bring down an opponent takes grabbing, dragging, reaching or whatever. That is OK. A defender has to do what he can—but most tactics only have the effect of a slap. If a defender aligns himself correctly, from the bottom of his feet all the way through his forehead, then he can leverage himself. When he uncoils, he has the power to knock someone out, or at least down. As it should be, using a fist is illegal in football, so I gained leverage with my helmet.

When I was at Baylor, I broke 16 helmets. Most of the damage happened when an opposing team was in a third- or fourth-and-one situation. On those plays, the other guy's runner usually rams straight ahead. The only way to stop him is to hit him head on. There should be a warning-label that reads, "Do not attempt this at home" or "For use by professionals only." If not done properly, this is one of the most dangerous parts of the game.

When a runner comes through the line of scrimmage head-on, it's difficult to force a fumble because the runner is usually bent over with the ball tucked away. A defender has to hit the first thing that he sees. That's usually the other guy's helmet. I have gone head-to-head with the best, and I loved it.

I loved cracking helmets.

I looked for someone who might rebuild the wall of righteousness that guards the land. I searched for someone to stand in the gap (Ezek. 22:30).

In World War II, during the Battle of the Bulge, the Germans had the U.S. 101st Airborne Division totally surrounded, and they issued an ultimatum for the Americans to surrender. General Anthony McAuliffe had been napping when the note of capitulation was delivered. A bit groggy, he first thought the Germans wanted to surrender to him. Now that is confidence!

When McAuliffe finally understood that the Germans wanted him to unconditionally surrender to them, he said, "Nuts!" The Germans didn't understand, so McAuliffe's associate, Colonel Bud Harper, clarified, telling the Nazis where they could go.[1] I don't condone bad language, but you have to admire the moxie. Those men stood in the gap and eventually won the war.

"A few good men" was a Marine Corps recruiting slogan. They don't use it anymore because it's not politically correct, but they knew a few good men were better than a bunch of mediocre ones. Indeed, a few good men and women can change the world.

Jesus knew this truth. He started with 11 good men, plus one that didn't make the cut. The 11 were so committed that some of them were martyred.[2] In fact, it's probable that only John reached old age.[3] Eleven totally committed men stood in the gap and changed the world.

In Ezekiel's day, God was looking for someone to stand in the gap. When Isaiah realized God was looking for a few good people, the prophet said, "Lord, I'll go! Send me."[4]

What's the key to being sent into the gap? Leverage.

When we have to go into battle helmet-to-helmet, courage is one quality that will give us the leverage we need. James gives us some other clues. He said that when we submit to God, draw near Him and humble ourselves before Him, we gain an advantage. When we do these things, God exalts us. In other words, we are given the leverage to stand in the gap and crack some helmets.

Time to start cracking.

Glorious God Who Wins All Battles, I am ready to crack some helmets. Thank You for giving me leverage through the forgiveness of my sins and thank You for allowing me to be Your servant. I want to stand in the gap for You. Here I am, Lord. I'll go! Send me.

TODAY'S READING: EZEKIEL 22:30; PSALM 143:10; ISAIAH 6:8; ROMANS 6:12-13; JAMES 4:1-10

Cheap Shots

I loved clean hits. I'd go full tilt but I'd always play fair. Whatever I had to do within the boundaries of the rules, I would do. That is playing with integrity.

Some guys didn't play fair. They would try to knock an opposing quarterback out of a game by driving their helmet into the quarterback's ribs when his arm was up. That's a cheap shot. Other players would look to hit an opponent's knees—a football player's knees are his meal ticket. That's another cheap shot. If a player loses his knees, he loses his livelihood. I refused to take cheap shots. Players who slam their helmets into a quarterback's ribs or go after someone's knees not only lack class, but they also lack integrity.

If a guy had his back turned and if he wasn't part of the play, I wasn't going to hit him. That would have been a cheap shot. On the other hand, if the quarterback still had the ball, even though his back was to me, I'd knock the snot out of him—that was what I was supposed to do. I would hit him hard, but high—I would not hit him low. I would hit him right.

Once I accidentally hit an opponent the wrong way and hurt him, but the referee didn't make the call. I knew I had broken a rule, so I told the ref, "I did it. I didn't do it on purpose but I did it. It was my fault. You should penalize me." I wanted both the referee and the other player to know that I was honest and that I would take responsibility for my mistakes. The ref thought I was nuts. If Buddy Ryan had known, he would have yanked me back to the sidelines. I don't even want to think about what Ditka would have said.

Not many players ask to be penalized when they violate a rule, but that's the way I tried to play. I wanted to win, but above all, I wanted to compete at the highest level. And to compete at the highest level, a person can't be taking cheap shots. I wanted to be a man of integrity—a man of character.

The LORD knows I shouldn't have done it," he said to his men. "It is a serious thing to attack the LORD's anointed one, for the LORD himself has chosen him (1 Sam. 24:6).

To a cheap-shot player, small offenses are no big deal. But to people of integrity, there are no small issues. Most players who aren't penalized for a cheap shot smile and think, *I got away with one.* But Mike didn't think that way. He was sorry about his mistake and fessed up.

King David never played in the NFL, but I wonder, would he have played with integrity? Would he have admitted to an error? Or would he have taken cheap shots and tried to get away with rules violations? Let's look at what he did when he had an opportunity to get away with one.

Saul, who was still king, was traveling with 3,000 men. He wanted to find David and kill him. David was hiding in a cave when Saul stopped and went inside the cave to relieve himself.[1] What a silhouette! I don't know how David and his men kept straight faces.

"Now is your opportunity," one of David's men whispered in his ear.[2]

So, David sneaked up close; but instead of cutting Saul's throat, he snipped off a piece of the king's robe and let the ruler finish his business, none the wiser. Immediately God told David that clipping the cloak was a cheap shot against someone who was appointed and anointed (Saul, like all of Israel's kings of that era, was God's chosen leader). David immediately felt sorry, not because he didn't kill Saul, but because he didn't honor the king.

"What's up with that?" his men queried.[3]

David repented and confessed to his men, "The Lord knows I shouldn't have done it [shown disrespect] . . . It is a serious thing to attack the Lord's anointed one."[4]

David made an about-face. As long as Saul was king, David showed him respect. With God, there are no cheap shots, nor can we get away with the little things. Recognizing this and living it out is a first step toward becoming a person of integrity.

Are you a cheap-shot player or a person of character?

Great God of Integrity, I want to be a person of character. When I am tempted to make a cutting remark, gossip or take any kind of cheap shot at another person, remind me to choose integrity instead. I want to honor life, Lord. Give me a deep regard for Your anointed ones. Thank You.

TODAY'S READING: 1 SAMUEL 24; PSALMS 25:21; 26:1; 101:2; MICAH 6:6-8; 1 CORINTHIANS 10:23-24; 1 PETER 4:7-11

Hit Like a Christian

Some people think the term "Christian football player" is an oxymoron. There are those who declare, "You're hurting people. You're knocking people out. How can you do that and call yourself a Christian?" Clearly these people don't understand competitive sports, and they might not understand Christianity.

Football is such a great game. It is one of the highest forms of competitive activity, and, yes, it's designed to be a contact sport. As I have noted, injuries happen. They are a part of the game.

But the focus should not be on who gets hurt; rather, it should be on how the game is played. There is a right way to play and there is a wrong way to play.

I could compete against anyone. It could be someone with whom I grew up in church or even someone who was my friend at school. No matter who the opponent was, I competed against him just like I would against somebody whom I didn't know. I always wanted to give my best, no matter who was on the other side of the line. When we do not give our best, we cheat God of His glory. God deserves our best, off the field and on the field. I have always felt that as Christian athletes, we should stand out from others by giving our best effort and perfecting our craft.

I was not really concerned about winning games. Yes, I wanted to win, but I always felt that if I did my best it would usually be good enough to win. Instead of focusing on the score, I'd focus on being the best I could be. That's acting like a Christian, too.

After a game was over, I could often tell an opponent, "Hey, I appreciated the contact. I appreciated the way you played." The tougher the competitor, the more I liked it. The better the opposition was, the greater the opportunity there was to improve myself.

The NFL is a rough and tough world, but there is a place for Christians within the fraternity of players. Just like in other areas of life, we bring a measure of integrity to the table.

Work hard and cheerfully at whatever you do, as though you were working for the Lord rather than for people (Col. 3:23).

"Work hard and cheerfully at whatever you do"[1] was Paul's mandate to slaves. We can substitute "workers" for "slaves" and not violate the text. The apostle wanted us to know that the Lord is our ultimate boss and we shouldn't cheat Him by doing less than our best. This means that when the game is all about hitting, Christian players should do their best to be the best hitters, but always within the framework of the rules.

This noted, there are times when we shouldn't do our best. Mercy occasionally demands that we back off a bit. Remember Mike's story about blowing out the Cowboys and the quarterback, Danny White, who was beat up? Mike asked his guys to lighten up and finish the game. There was no cause to crush, hurt or rub Cowboy noses in their loss. That's why when a game is out of reach, an unwritten rule calls upon coaches to pull the starters and put in third stringers.

No coach will tell his players to give less than 100 percent, but yanking the starters effectively eases an opponent's bruised ego. The third stringers should still give 100 percent, but their best isn't as good as the starters' best.

Some coaches don't pull their starters and grudges follow. Running up the score is generally considered in poor taste. A coach with class doesn't do it.

We should cheerfully work hard at whatever we do but be compassionate as we do it. That's our Christian principle. Some coaches think that's being soft. There is one NBA coach who fines his players $5,000 if they help an opposing player get up off the floor. I don't like that policy. I enjoyed reaching down and helping guys up, especially if I had knocked them down.

Whatever our arena of influence—stadium, office, classroom or assembly line—it is our responsibility to bring integrity to the table. If we play a contact sport, the opposition will be more interested in our Jesus if we hit them as hard as we can and then help them up.

Great Provider, thank You for giving me meaningful things to do. I want to learn to give my best as an offering to You. Show me how to give my all and be as compassionate as Your Son, my Lord Jesus Christ. Thank You.

TODAY'S READING: PSALM 119:2,34; MATTHEW 5:13-16; 1 CORINTHIANS 10:23—11:1; COLOSSIANS 3:22-25

A Melting Pot

When I was a kid, Roger Staubach was my hero. He played quarterback for Dallas. Even when the Cowboys were behind, I knew that he could pull it out. I just knew it. I had other heroes, too, but Roger was my man. I suppose it's unusual for a boy of color from the ghetto to have a Caucasian hero, but I've always tried to be fair-minded when it comes to race.

The high school I attended was overwhelmingly African American. One year, two Caucasian kids came. I remember standing up for the two boys when my classmates picked on them—I even sat with them during lunch. Race was never an issue for my parents, so it was never one for me either.

In my family, we never referred to anyone of any race as "those people." What I heard from my parents was "We have to do what's right in God's eyes, so we're not going to worry about any differences."

My dad never played the race card, and he didn't like it when other people did. He talked with everyone in the same way, no matter his or her skin color. He'd look straight into the person's eyes and have a conversation.

Perhaps my family was so equal-minded because of our melting-pot roots. On my father's side, my great-grandfather was German. On my mom's side, my great-grandmother was Native American, and my great-grandfather was Mexican. This mix literally makes me a melting pot.

Since I was raised to treat everyone the same, I was surprised when I discovered that skin color was still a hot button in a lot of churches. It shouldn't be. We're one Body in Christ. I think that Jesus would confront the problem head on. I can almost hear Him say, "If you've got a problem with white, black, Mexican or any other people, change or get out! Don't return until your attitude is fixed." Race isn't an issue in heaven, so why is it one here?

Then Peter replied, "I see very clearly that God doesn't show partiality. In every nation he accepts those who fear him and do what is right" (Acts 10:34-35).

Peter's parents were not from the Ozarks and he did not live in a trailer park, but he no doubt was around plenty of racial bad-mouthing. Peter was a big, rough-talking, red-knecked fisherman—the kind of guy that you might see in a World Wrestling Federation skirmish. Like all Jews of his time, he divided people into two groups. There were God's chosen people and there was everyone else, called gentiles. Jews of Peter's day didn't go into gentiles' homes, didn't eat with gentiles, talked to them publicly only when necessary, never socialized with them, and certainly never married one. This was deeply entrenched prejudice. This social norm explains why it was such a big deal when God sent Peter to the house of the gentile Cornelius.

It's not easy for anyone to put aside the prejudices that he or she has been taught. It's not easy to do an about-face, even when God makes His stand clear in a vision, which is exactly what He did for Peter. God got Peter's attention, told him to go downstairs and to go with three men who were about to knock on the door. Just as God said, the men knocked and the next day Peter went into the house of a gentile. Once there, Peter led Cornelius's entire household to Christ, and overcame his racial prejudice at the same time. (Isn't it amazing how God does that!)

Peter was one of the first Jews of his day to discover that God was no respecter of persons. Gentiles were just as important to the Father as Jews were. It was a tough pill to swallow, but to Peter's credit, he swallowed it— and then he went to the elders of the Early Church and told them what God had done.

The race issue was settled for Peter, but sadly not everyone in the Early Church followed his lead. Long-held prejudices were never totally dislodged, much like what happens in the Church today.

Mike Singletary asks a good question: Why is race an issue with any Christian? It is not one with God.

Holy Father of Us All, show me any lingering lies that still dwell in my mind and help me to love all people as Your Son loves them. Please use me to be a part of purging prejudice from Your church, to the glory of Jesus Christ my Lord. Amen.

TODAY'S READING: ACTS 10:1–11:18; GALATIANS 3:23–4:7; 1 CORINTHIANS 12:12-14

It would be nice if we could pick when we get a fever, the flu or a cold. Obviously we can't. This fact of life is of no comfort to a football player. Waking up sick before a game is the worst of scenarios. It happened to me once.

We were playing the Washington Redskins. I was as ill as I have ever been. The day before the game, I had vertigo and was vomiting. I had to crawl to the bathroom and spent the day turning myself inside out. The room would not stop spinning.

I wasn't any better the next morning, so I called our trainer in a panic: "Freddy, I can't get out of bed. If I get up, I'll fall down."

Freddy suggested that I sit out the Redskins game.

"No way!" I exclaimed. "I'm going to play. I don't know how, but I'm going to play today."

I called my teammate Shaun Gayle and asked him to take me to the stadium. On the way to the game, I told Shaun, "I don't know how I'm going to play today. All I know is that on every play I need you to say, 'Greater is He who is in me, than he who is in the world.' If you say that, I think I'll make it."

I was serious. As I was talking, my vision was so blurred that I saw three Shauns. In fact, I saw three of everything.

I was still seeing in threes when I went onto the field. During the game, I just hit whatever was in the middle. After each play, Shaun would grab me and say, "Mike, greater is He who is in you than he who is in the world." He did it after every play, the entire game. Sometimes I prodded him: "Come on, Shaun, say it louder." He screamed, "Greater is He who is in you than he who is in the world!"

I know it's hard to believe, but that was one of the best games I played that year. There was no question about how great God was—and is.

Greater is He who is in you than he who is in the world (1 John 4:4, *NASB*).

Never ask an old man how he's feeling. The conversation will turn into an organ recital. I'm feeling that way because my God-got-me-through-it story came during a hospital stay, not a great athletic performance.

I burned out in my first full-time ministry position. Stress had led to a respiratory condition. I found myself in a hospital room, hooked up to breathing machines and on morphine part of the time, but still leading a Bible study.

Five ambulatory patients and a nurse attended the study for five days. The nurse and one of the patients accepted Christ as Savior. A doctor heard about the study and was so blown away by what God did that he rededicated his life to God. We had a revival in the hospital. God was great in me, even in the midst of my incredible weakness.[1]

The Lord also strengthened the apostle Paul. Paul had a physical problem he called a thorn in the flesh. I'm guessing it was an eye problem that came about as a result of being blinded on the Damascus Road or of being stoned (with rocks, not drugs). Paul alluded to God fixing everything except his eyes. I am not sure whether he saw three of everything like Mike did, but three times the apostle prayed for healing. Each time God spoke: "My gracious favor is all you need. My power works best in your weakness."[2] Through Paul's weakness, God changed the world. Weakness makes us get out of the way so God can do His thing through us.

We all have issues. We get sick. We are stressed. At times, we have had it with the world. That's OK. When we are at our weakest, we are in a perfect position for God to be at His greatest.

Great God of Ultimate Power, I offer the gift of my weakness to You today. I'm not trying to put You to a test; rather, I ask that You encourage me by showing Your greatness through my weakness. Thank You.

TODAY'S READING: 2 CORINTHIANS 12:1-10

Wounded Knee

No player wants to intentionally cause a serious injury to another player, but it happens. I am not referring to scratches and bruises—everyone gets banged up. I am not even talking about being momentarily knocked silly. By serious injury, I mean a time when a guy is hit and can't get up. That's major.

Whenever a player went down—and stayed down—or if a stretcher was brought in, the game was immediately on pause for me. I could not continue until the injured person got the attention he needed. In fact, I would lay hands on him or pray silently, even if he was an opposing player. I'd ask God to heal him. I'd pray for his wife, his mom, his career and his livelihood. That may seem foolish but prayer works.

Thankfully, I never suffered a career-threatening injury. But in 1987, I pinched off the end of my finger, which wasn't a big deal, and I damaged my knee, which could have been major. Both injuries happened in Minnesota's MetroDome on one of the worst turfs in the world. Against the Vikings, I tweaked my knee when I attempted to simultaneously turn and hit a player. I walked off the pain and finished the game—but the knee wasn't right.

I was working out one day at the start of the next season when my knee suddenly popped. The doctors discovered a piece of cartilage floating around in the joint. I probably should have had an operation to fix it but that would have ended my season. Instead, I prayed, *Lord, let me make it through the season and I will give You the glory.*

On some days, my knee hurt so much that I could barely practice. Yet on game day, I had no pain. No pain! During any given game, I didn't know what my knee might do, so I rode on faith. After the season, I had the fragment removed.

That year, I was the NFL Player of the Year for the second time. It was the best year that I've ever had in football. I still give God the glory.

Our dedication to Christ makes us look like fools, but you are so wise! We are weak, but you are so powerful! You are well thought of, but we are laughed at (1 Cor. 4:10).

It is easy to look foolish. Our friends trick us on April 1. We walk out of the bathroom with toilet paper affixed to the bottom of one shoe. We convince ourselves that the hottie is attracted to us when all she wants is to know what time it is. How embarrassing!

With equal ease we can not only be embarrassed, but we also can actually be downright foolish. In a rush to get to church, we speed down the highway and yell at the kids in the backseat. We fall for the latest get-rich-quick scheme. We cheat on a spouse. How foolish!

Sometimes we cheat on God, too. How doubly foolish!!

Nonetheless, when it comes to fools and foolishness the Bible poses a paradox. The apostle Paul promised that Christ would make us look like fools.[1] Christ's kind of foolishness is not foolhardy, but it can be embarrassing. In fact, it is something to which we should aspire. What is up with that?

There was a woman in my church who had Multiple Sclerosis. God made it clear: I was to pray with her. So, with the elders at my side, I put my hands on her shoulders and I asked God to heal her. Nothing happened. She was not cured, nor, to my knowledge, has she improved since then. Was I a flat-footed fool, or was I a fool for Christ?

Job lost everything and looked pretty foolish. When he asked God what was up, God basically told him to shush up. God reasoned that we do not know everything about this world, so how can we understand all of God's ways?

We, of course, have slivers of insight, but sometimes we have to be content to appear as fools. God sustained Mike's wounded knee, but He did not heal the woman with M.S. Why one and not the other? I don't really want God to answer. I probably wouldn't understand. I'll just trust Him, fall on my knees and keep praying—even if I look foolish in the process. Hopefully, I will be a fool for Christ's sake.

Heavenly Healer, thank You for the times when You choose to heal us. And thank You for Your greater plan when You don't. I will trust You and I will continue to pray. Go ahead, let me be a fool for Christ's sake.

TODAY'S READING: 1 CORINTHIANS 4:6-14; 2 CORINTHIANS 12:9-10; PHILIPPIANS 1:27—2:2

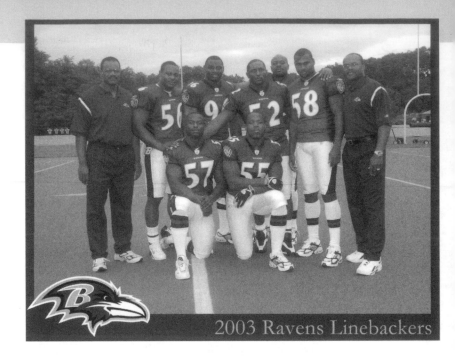

2003 Ravens Linebackers

Back in the game. I[n] 2003, Mike joined th[e] staff of the Baltimor[e] Ravens as linebacker[s] coach (above). Two y[ears] later, he moved on t[o] San Francisco 49ers (right).

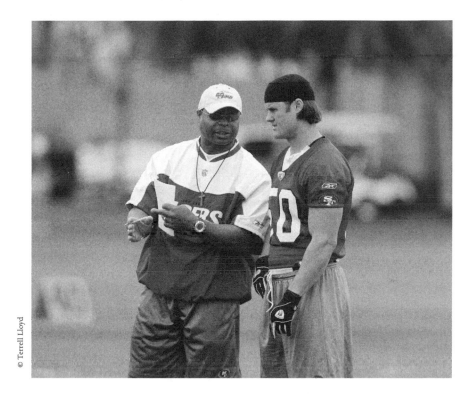

Getting ready. In a preseason minicamp, Mike talks strategy with 49ers linebacker Derek Smith (above) and brings out his machine (below), which makes practice more efficient.

SINGLETARY COMMENTARY

Wounded Ego

My worst day in the NFL came in 1989 against the Tampa Bay Buccaneers. I was playing the game of my life—in fact, I had already knocked a guy out cold. That was actually a little scary. He was out a bit too long. I even prayed for him.

I had so much confidence that I didn't care whom I went up against. It didn't matter how big the other guy was—he was going down. I was downright cocky. I told my teammate Richard Dent, "You know what? When they play against me, they'll say they came against the best. No one has ever run over me. Never!"

It was true. I had never been knocked on my back, and I was outright prideful about it.

Toward the end of the fourth quarter, Tampa Bay was behind, but the Buccaneers drove down the field, ready to score and win the game. James Wilder was Tampa's running back. I respect him a lot. He was one of the best backs ever.

Wilder caught a pass from Vinny Testaverde and ran toward the sideline. He wanted to get out of bounds to stop the clock and give the Bucs enough time to score. I told myself, *Don't let him run out of bounds. When you tackle him, lie on him and let the clock run out.*

Instead of running toward Wilder to hit him, I ran up to grab him. I was on my heels when Wilder turned up field and put his head down. Bam! He knocked me over—flat on my back—and gave Tampa the momentum.

It was the first and only time I was ever run over.

Tampa Bay won the game on that play and it was one of my most embarrassing moments. I kept my mouth closed after that. I had learned that, indeed, pride does come before the fall.

First pride, then the crash—the bigger the ego, the harder the fall (Prov. 16:18, *THE MESSAGE*).

Mike's story reminds me of Haman and Absalom.

Haman's goal in life was to get Mordecai, a Jewish man, to bow down to him. Everything else became meaningless. Try as Haman might, he couldn't force or coerce Mordecai to even bend one knee. Haman was so fixated on his warped passion that he decided to kill Mordecai—and for good measure, he would kill all of Mordcai's people, too. Haman even built gallows for the purpose.

This Haman was a proud man who boasted and bragged a bunch.[1] He even stopped to toot his own horn before he captured Mordecai, or any Jewish person. In the end, Haman found himself on his heels with a rope around his neck falling through the trap door in the gallows he built.

Absalom had a pride problem, too. He didn't draw attention to himself by cranking up the bass on his high-tech boomer in his chariot; rather, he had an entourage of fifty men who preceded him and announced his arrival. The boy had pride issues. Absalom didn't just want to take over the kingdom; he wanted to rub his dad's (David's) nose in the mud and the sludge as he went.[2]

Like Haman, Absalom got ahead of himself. While escaping from an adversary on his horse, Absalom's hair got tangled in a limb, causing him to come off his steed and dangle in a tree until his enemy killed him.

Don't get ahead of yourself. Don't toot your own horn. Let others speak of your accomplishments, lest your horn becomes a kazoo.

Great God and Father, You delight in humility. Oh Lord, I want to rejoice and recount Your greatness. I choose to sing Your praises. I don't want to take anything away from You. All glory belongs to You. Help me to remember to pass any praise that comes to me directly on to You. Thank You.

Midnight

Offensive linemen, quarterbacks and kickers can play into their late thirties or early forties, but not linebackers. There have been a few exceptions to that rule, but not many.

I was 34 when I first noticed my skills diminishing. I had just been to the Pro Bowl again, but it was much more difficult to prepare for the upcoming season. In years past, I had looked forward to training. That year, it was a chore. I knew that my time as a linebacker was running out.

Reality hit me around mid-season. During my entire career, when I hit someone his weight didn't matter, he went down. Not on this particular day. I hit an opposing rookie just right, but he remained upright. Two or three times during the game, I got a lick on him. Bam! Bam! But the guy kept pushing back.

After the game, my coach and I looked at the film. My coach said, "Mike, you hit that guy pretty good." I told myself, *If you only knew—I can't bring the wood any more.*

I had watched other players try to stay in the game beyond their prime. Some continued to play because they loved the game. Others just needed the paycheck. I loved to play football, but I also loved the game so much that I didn't want to dishonor it by continuing to play at a lower level. I didn't want to play, saying, "I used to be able to do this" or "I remember when I could do that."

I knew that I could have played two or three more years, especially if I was surrounded by talented players. But Chicago was rebuilding. It would have been tough.

I had felt like a Cinderella player all along. Even to have played at Baylor and in the NFL was a miracle—I was the least likely person to have the shoe fit. But I gave my best. I played almost every down at a very high level for 12 wonderful years. However, time was running out. The clock had struck 12. It was time to quit.

He must become greater and greater, and I must become less and less (John 3:30).

For Mike Singletary, playing professional football was not a fairy tale; rather, it was a dream that came true. When midnight arrived, he chose to leave the dream world most people only imagine. For the first time in his life he lived an ordinary life—at least as ordinary as it would ever get for Mike.

John the Baptist made a similar shift at about the same age.

John was earthy. He didn't dress well. Coarse and scratchy clothes made of the cheapest camel hair adorned his body. John dressed like a prophet who never made a profit. His diet consisted of bugs and honey. He lived like a backpacker, looked like a wild man and snacked on locusts.

This desert man from the priestly line of Aaron was a hard-nosed son of the sand. He specialized in getting in your face. There was no compromise in him and he was never accused of being the life of the party. His specialties were fasting and prayer. The masses loved him but the puckered, righteous Pharisaical leaders hated him. Such a response was to be expected. John called them a "brood of snakes."[1]

Jesus thought highly of John. He called John the greatest man ever born.[2] Coming from the Son of God, that's quite a compliment. When you are All-Pro and number one in God's Hall of Fame, you've had a good run. But when John hit his mid-thirties, it was time to change course. "He [Jesus] must increase, I must decrease," John said.[3] The Baptizer knew when it was time to step aside and pass the torch. Someone greater was on the scene.

I don't find retirement noted in the Bible. The concept is mostly a waste of valuable time and resources. I do not plan on retiring. Instead—as my health and energy level decline—I will adjust. I will gladly trade airplanes, hotels and rental cars for peace at home and my computer. I'll keep doing what I can.

Just because our clock strikes twelve, it doesn't mean that we should stop pointing people to Jesus.

Holy God of Love, regardless of my age or circumstances, I want to serve You and point people to Jesus Christ. As my life takes its course, as my sinful past takes its toll, and as Your will comes to pass, I pledge whatever I have to You. My energy and my possessions are Yours. Amen.

Lights On

As a kid I watched a lot of scary movies. I especially liked horror flicks. Some of them were downright evil, with vampires and witches. Add to that a lot of bad things in my neighborhood and the bickering between my mom and dad in the house, and it isn't a surprise that I ended up being afraid of the dark.

Calling what I felt "a fear of the dark" is probably an overstatement. Yet, I felt a lot more comfortable with light than I did with darkness. As recently as a few years ago, whenever I would travel, at night—out of habit—I'd turn on the bathroom light. I was just more comfortable going to sleep with some light in the room.

Why would a grown man who loves God have even a modicum of fear for the dark? I've always had a great respect for the Lord, even when I wasn't following Him. At the same time, I had an unhealthy respect for the evil one. I feared the enemy too much.

In more recent years, the Lord has shown me that I should not respect the devil at all and that I do need to fear him. I've discovered that Satan fears me more than any opposing quarterback ever feared the Chicago defense. As long as I claim the blood of Jesus, walk in faith and stand for Christ, I have nothing of which to be afraid. I know that God is in total control.

I took another step. I also prayed back the ground that I gave away when I was a kid watching those movies and living in fear. By "praying back ground," I simply mean that I applied the blood of Jesus to any lingering ill effect those episodes early in my life might still have on me.

I'm still more comfortable with light. When I wake up in the morning, I like all the lights on, but there are now times when I prefer to be in the dark. I sit, relax and breathe in calmness. That's new for me. The Lord has brought me peace.

I have come as a light to shine in this dark world, so that all who put their trust in me will no longer remain in the darkness (John 12:46).

It's not unusual to be afraid of the dark, especially for children. Prayer always brings calmness and peace. In Christ, we have no reason to fear, but darkness has a mystique about it.

Spiritual assaults often occur at night. Darkness is the hiding place for evil.[1] By this I mean that the enemy will often attack at night when we are tired. But also there is something about actual darkness. Wiccan ceremonies often occur after sunset and we all have heard stories about what happens under a full moon. Satan and the dark side go hand in hand.

By contrast, God always associates Himself with light. God brought light into darkness at creation. Jesus is the light that came into the world. The Holy Spirit is the light that illuminates our soul.

Physical light is made up of three distinct rays. Each ray has its own function. The first, often called invisible light, is neither seen nor felt. The second is both seen and felt. The third is not seen but is felt as heat.[2] The Trinity exists as three—yet, like light, they are one.

Not only does light illustrate the Trinity, but it also reflects God's unchanging constant character. Einstein was able to construct the theory of relativity because the speed of light is the only measurable constant in our physical, material universe.[3] Similar to the speed of light, God is the same yesterday, today and forever[4]—and He shines everywhere.

God's light can shine in the darkest of places, including the ugliest and most depressing of places—what the Bible calls the valley of the shadow of death.[5] Even in the hardest place, believers can find relief from the dark, because God is light. God's Word lights the way.[6]

A believer has reason to be cautious in the dark, but there is no reason to fear it.

Great God of Purest Light, I rejoice at the thought of darkness fleeing before You. Would You shine in the darkest parts of my being? Would You brighten the shadows of my soul? I invite You to illuminate every nook and cranny of my deceitful heart. Then, allow me to reflect the light of Jesus Christ. Thank You.

TODAY'S READING: PSALMS 23; 119:105; JOHN 3:18-21; ROMANS 13:11-14; EPHESIANS 6:11-20; COLOSSIANS 1:9-14; 1 JOHN 2:7-11

A Miraculous Moment

I know that God has miraculously intervened in my life many times. Most of the time, I probably did not even know He had acted. On three occasions, I knew He had.

One miracle occurred when I was still playing football. I tried to avoid vulnerable situations that might cause an injury; but on one particular play against the Houston Oilers, I jumped over a pile of players and landed on the outside part of my foot just as another player was coming down toward my knee. In my mind, the sequence happened in slow motion. I could see the other guy coming, but I couldn't avoid contact. Expecting to be injured, I screamed, "Ohhh!"

I resigned myself to a major injury. In that split second, I could see my career ending. But nothing happened—absolutely nothing. It was as if an angel grabbed the other player and moved him, or moved my knee. It was amazing. Instantly I knew that God had miraculously intervened. I yelled, "Oh, Lord! Jesus, thank You!"

When I watched our game film the next day, I looked closely at the play. I wanted to see what God had done, but all I could see was a pile of players, including me. Nonetheless, I knew what had happened. It was a miraculous moment.

I can't explain why God would spare me while others more deserving than me sometimes get injured. Perhaps God was good to me because my mom prayed so much. She prayed when I was young, when I was drafted and while I played. She never missed a day—and I could feel her prayers.

I thank God that I had a mom who prayed, and I also thank Him for intervening on my behalf.

For the Scriptures tell us, "Abraham believed God, so God declared him to be righteous" (Rom. 4:3).

In Isaac's day, some people offered a firstborn son as a sacrifice. God decided to use this practice as a test for Abraham and his son Isaac.

God instructed Abraham to collect Isaac, some wood and enough food for a three-day trek. Both father and son knew that they would be called upon to make a sacrifice to God. When they arrived at their destination, they built an altar and prepared the sacrifice—which was to be Isaac.

God had made a string of promises to Abraham, promises that could only come true if Isaac were alive. The seed of the future Messiah was to come through Isaac, and Isaac's descendents were to establish an enduring nation that would bless the world. Despite the contradiction, Abraham had faith that God could do what appeared to be impossible.

When we tell this well-worn Old Testament story, we tend to focus on Abraham and his faith. What about Isaac? He carried the wood to be used in the sacrifice, so he had to be big enough to take out his father, who must have been about 115 years old at the time. Could it be that Isaac believed, too, and consented to what his father was about to do? Like Mike had on that play in the Oilers' game, Isaac could see the sacrifice unfolding. His father, Abraham, was about to kill him—and there was absolutely nothing he could do to stop it from happening. Perhaps Isaac was resolved to a life-ending injury.

We know how the story ends. God intervened and provided a different sacrifice. Certainly, Abraham and Isaac both gave thanks. And, as was predicted, the Messiah did come from Isaac's lineage, and the great people of Israel still thrive to this day, blessing all other nations. We know of Abraham's faith, but perhaps Isaac had great faith, too.

Intervention by God is wonderful. When is the last time He stepped in for you? Did you give Him the thanks He deserves?

Dear God of Miracles, thank You for the times when, on my behalf, You step in and alter the normal course of events. I know there are occasions when You intervene and I am not aware. I thank You for those times, too. Please accept my gratitude and praise. Thank You for Your protection. Amen.

TODAY'S READING: GENESIS 22:1-19; ROMANS 4:1—5:11; HEBREWS 11:8-12

Called to Coach

If I had gone into coaching before now, I'd probably be divorced. I wouldn't have had the knowledge or maturity I needed.

For starters, I wouldn't have seen that I don't have to sacrifice my family. It has taken time for me to learn how to balance my life, how to be passionate about something but not disregard other important things, too. Previously, I would have been absorbed with coaching instead of focusing on my identity as a man of God, a husband and a father. Being a coach can happen only after I have these parts of my life in order.

Coaching then becomes a vehicle that allows me to pass on what I've learned. Many players are searching, begging for a man to say, "This is who you are. There's greatness in you. There are great things for you to do. It's in you. I'll help you find it. We'll find it together. It's time for you to be the man God created you to be."

Being a man has nothing to do with drugs, alcohol or loose women. These will only get a person into trouble. Being a man isn't about scoring touchdowns and knocking people down. A football player will make big plays, earn a lot of money and have fame, but these can't be his identity.

When I talk with young men, I see a light go on in their eyes. This blesses me, because I know that beyond coaching, helping people is what God has called me to do. He wants me to shepherd young men. I fought being a pastor and I fought being a coach. Clearly, God wants me to be both.

God spoke to me in my spirit and said, *Humble yourself. You don't have to be the head coach right now. I just want you where you are. Are you willing to be effective where I call you? I will prepare you for the right time, but your heart's got to be right.*

"What do You mean by my heart having to be right?" I asked.

God said, *You've got too much pride. It's not about you, Mike. It's about Me.*

You have heard me teach many things that have been confirmed by many reliable witnesses. Teach these great truths to trustworthy people who are able to pass them on to others (2 Tim. 2:2).

We have to pay our dues on the way to the top, especially when God calls us to go there. There are always sharp edges of pride to be filed. Even Paul was an assistant for a while.

After Paul's conversion to Christianity, he had what is called a wilderness time. For three years, Paul was in Arabia. We assume that he was studying, praying and getting ready to rumble. He finished this period ready to be a head coach.

Believers are called to coach. In the Church we call it discipleship. Assistant coaches develop players. Head coaches turn individuals into teams. No one was a better head coach in the New Testament Church than was Paul.

The great apostle would have been a fabulous quarterback. Paul was a master at handing off ministries and was unsurpassed at passing responsibilities on to people whom he had mentored. During three missionary journeys, Paul established a string of churches across most of the known world. Each church contained people whom the apostle had discipled.

I counted 23 people in the New Testament who were discipled by coach Paul. Many of those whom he coached later coached others. Titus went to Crete and Dalmatia. Timothy went to Corinth and Ephesus. Tychius went to Ephesus and then on to Colossi. Crescens went to Galatia. Phoebe went to Rome. John Mark went to Cyprus. And the list goes on. It's amazing what one coach can do.

How did Paul do it? Look at Acts 20:17-38 for some clues. Paul wrote spiritual prescriptions. He kept his men trying new ideas and ministries until they discovered their gifts. He taught the basics of the faith: Word, worship, prayer, giving and outreach. He challenged them by throwing them into tough situations. He was confrontational, but in love. He cut them loose, made them independent. He commissioned them for service, bestowed his blessing and, in most cases, gave them a flock to shepherd.

God has called you to coach. After He files you down a bit, you might even be a head coach. Go for it!

Oh God of Wonder, I am humbled to think that You would
count on me to accomplish Your purposes in the lives of those whom
You love. Alone I am not up to the task, but with You, I can do it.
I will coach Your children in the faith. Amen.

TODAY'S READING: ACTS 20:17-38; PHILIPPIANS 3:17—4:1; 2 TIMOTHY 2:1-13

God's Moves

God told my wife, Kim, that I was going to coach, so I started praying about it, too. I was reading my Bible and I started thinking out loud, "Lord, why are You calling me to this now? What is this about?" I asked the Lord to speak to me.

In my spirit, I heard, *Mike, it's not about you. It's about Me. Are you willing to do what I'm asking you to do? Son, are you willing to be blessed?*

"Yes, Lord, I am," I said out loud.

Are you willing to be blind? Are you willing to be foolish for Me?

"Sure, Lord."

I called the Bears first and said, "I want you to know I'm not asking for a job. But out of respect for you and the organization, I'm calling you first to let you know that I'm going to be coaching. If there is room, if I'm supposed to be there, call me back. If there is not, that's fine, too."

When the Bears declined I said, "Please, don't even explain it. I knew if it was supposed to work it would. Thank you, I'm going to move on."

Kim and I started packing because we knew that we wouldn't be in Chicago for too much longer. I started calling other head coaches. Again, I didn't ask for a job. I just told them I was going to coach and that I was available.

I didn't know if I was going to coach at a high school, a college or in the NFL. I hadn't called the Ravens but out of the blue I got a call from Coach Brian Billick on a Thursday. I interviewed on Saturday. Kim flew in on Sunday and pronounced, "You know what? This is it!" We sold our house in four days. I agreed to a contract that Tuesday. I was coaching that Friday. My family came east to Baltimore a month later. Isn't that just like God?

Sometimes God moves quickly, so we have to be ready.

Then the LORD told Abram, "Leave your country, your relatives, and your father's house, and go to the land that I will show you" (Gen. 12:1).

My first ministry role was directing a Christian Camp in the mountains of Southern California. But after five years, God led me to leave. I wanted to exit correctly, so I gave a six-month notice. There was a risk that the board would let me go on the spot, not wanting a lame-duck director. However, I knew it would take a while to find a replacement and I didn't want them to be without a director, unless they wanted it that way.

There was no question that God had led my wife and me to run the camp. We had even sold our home so that we couldn't go back to Egypt, like the Israelites wanted to do when it got tough in the wilderness.[1] We were committed to following God's lead and we weren't going back, no matter how tough it got.

Well, it got real tough. Ministry isn't easy, especially for rookies. We got bruised, but it made us better. Our faith got close to faltering, but never did. God has been faithful. As we have followed His lead, doors have opened for me to write books.

Abraham followed God's lead, too. God told him to leave his land.[2] Didn't hearing from God make the decision a no-brainer? No. It wasn't easy for Abe, and it wasn't easy for my wife and me. We loved our church, our home and our wonderful friends. We are beach people. There wasn't anything for us in the mountains. But God told us to go there, just as he told Abraham to go to Haran. Then God told us to leave the mountains.

Abraham was 75 when he left. After Abraham's dad died, God told him to move again. This time He didn't say where to go. God also told Abraham that he would be the father of a great nation. Abraham was in his eighties and had no kids, but he still believed. So, he went and God did the rest.

Mike followed God and is coaching. I followed God and I am writing. Who knows what will happen to you if you follow God.

Heavenly Leader, be the light to my path. I chose to walk by faith, not by sight. Lead me. I want to follow. Thank You.

TODAY'S READING: GENESIS 12:1-5; PSALM 119:105,130; PROVERBS 6:23; ACTS 7:2-8; LUKE 6:46-49; 2 CORINTHIANS 5:1-10; HEBREWS 11:8-19

God's Got My Back

I have experienced God's protection. Going from being a sickly child to an NFL All-Pro was definitely His handiwork. I experienced God at work during a high school football game, too.

I was playing a game against a tough opponent and I felt like the opposing players were intentionally going after my knees, trying to hurt me. Finally, someone got me. Pow! My knee was smacked hard and it popped. Everybody heard it. The guys on the sideline said, "Oh, man! He's not going to get up."

I laid on the ground for a minute. At first I was frantic. It was painful! Finally, I prayed, "Lord, are You going to let me lie here? Let me get up and finish this game." I got up, started walking, began jogging, took off running and went back in the game.

Many years later when I was with the Bears, I got a package in the mail from the center I'd played against in that high school game. It contained a video clip of the play where my knee popped. In the enclosed letter the center said, "I want you to know, I didn't like what happened then and I still don't like it now. That's why I'm sending this to you. You were a great player and our coach said, 'Whatever you have to do, get him out of the game. Take his knees out.' I didn't want to do it but I felt I had no choice. However, I got to a point where I told the coach that I wouldn't do it. So, he pulled me and put the other center in. I just want you to know that I apologize for that night."

I said to myself, *I knew it!*

God had me covered, then and now. I saw Him at work back then during the game and through the mail when a man sought forgiveness. I suppose I could have missed it and called it something else, but I didn't. It was God at work. He had my back.

And we know that God causes everything to work together for the good of those who love God and are called according to his purpose for them (Rom. 8:28).

David didn't miss God's handiwork either. He didn't like it, but he didn't miss it. Yes, he got uppity and sinned some pretty big sins. Adultery and murder aren't as big as blaspheming God, but they probably come in somewhere on the top-ten-sins list.

Because David committed these sins, he suffered the consequences. Even though God took away the baby that resulted from David's sin, the king used the event to get back into fellowship with his maker. He didn't throw a fit or get angry with God; rather, David grieved, prayed and fasted while the child was sick, hoping that the infant would recover. When the child died, David was still thankful. How could he be thankful? David had already reconciled with God. After all of this had happened, David sat down and wrote Psalm 51.

God had David's back all along.

God causes everything to work together for the good of those who love Him and are called according to His purpose.[1] Everything that happens might not be good. David's baby had to die. But everything that took place was used by God to make some good come out of it. David repented, but he never would have if God hadn't had his back.

Look at a rose. Do you see the thorns or the blossom? Look at a glass of water. Is it half empty or half full? How you see things depends on how you look at them, and how you look at them depends on your walk with the Lord. David saw the blossom.

We can count on God to cover our back, too.

Dear Unrelenting Father, thank You for not giving up on me.
Thank You for pursuing me and not letting go. Thank You for
watching over me when I didn't care about You. Thank You for
bringing me to the point of both loving and giving myself to You.
You had my back all along. Thank You. Amen.

The Best Test

I played middle linebacker with an eye toward coaching. I always wanted to coach and planned on it—until I found out how much time being a coach took. Then I had second thoughts.

As a player, I had to work long hours during the season, but the load was lighter during the off-season. A coach can make his own hours, but he is always on the clock all year long. I have seven great kids and a wonderful wife. When my playing days were over, I decided that I wasn't going to sacrifice my family for the sake of the game. So I did not immediately pursue a coaching position.

I did talk with Baylor when the school was hiring a new head coach. Going back to my alma mater was appealing—and at the time I did think it was where God was calling me—but the school chose someone else, so that was that.

During the 1990s I spent my time becoming a better father and husband. I also further developed my ideas on leadership, speaking at seminars, writing, studying and observing. Sometimes the best tests come during times of preparation.

I am still in a time of preparation. When I was on staff with the Ravens, I wanted to be the best linebacker coach ever. Now with the 49ers, I want to be the best assistant head coach and linebacker coach ever. I will be the best that I can be.

When my turn comes to be a head coach, I will again do my best to be the best ever. Deep in my being, with everything that's in me, I believe I can be one of the best coaches in the history of the NFL. That's what I want to be. I've got a ways to go, but I am making strides. I believe it is my destiny.

I don't want to sound arrogant, but I believe that God has gifted me in this way. I know that if I do my best, being the best is the most likely result. When it happens, I will give God all the glory.

But if you are unwilling to serve the LORD, then choose today whom you will serve. Would you prefer the gods your ancestors served beyond the Euphrates? Or will it be the gods of the Amorites in whose land you now live? But as for me and my family, we will serve the Lord (Josh. 24:15).

Mike expects to be the best. Is that a good goal? Does it stand the biblical test?

Why does Mike want to excel? To find the answer we must look at Mike's heart. When he succeeds, who gets the glory? Mike or God?

Most people can't handle the highest arches of success. Mike got his first test as a star player. Of course, only Mike and God know for sure, but from all outward appearances, Mike aced the can-you-handle-success test. He gave God the glory. The point here is that it is a matter of the heart, not a matter of doing good works, or even saying the right thing. Let me explain.

There is a fine balance between faith and works. Works without faith are worthless. Faith without works doesn't pass the test either. Good works come out of a proper faith, but there is something wrong with our faith if there are no works. The faith/works teeter-totter balances on a single point. Do we think we are gaining God's favor by what we do? If we do, we missed the point.

God already loves us. Good works for points will never please Him. But wanting to become the best we can be to the glory of God will please Him every time.

If I understand Mike's heart right, he is serving as an apprentice to the glory of God until the Father gives him a head coaching job. Mike believes that if he can become all he is capable of becoming, he will be the best of all time. Whether that statement is evidence of confidence or not, only time will tell. For now he is happy to take on the tests of an apprentice.

If I understand Mike's heart right, when all is said and done, what he really wants to hear is for God to say, "Well done, my good and faithful servant."[1]

Great God Who Prepares Me for the Best, I want to excel and bring glory to You. Lead me to the place that You have for me and give me a faith that produces works to Your glory. Thank You.

TODAY'S READING: EXODUS 24:13-18; NUMBERS 27:15-20;
JOSHUA 17:8-13; 24:15, JAMES 2:14-26

A Messenger

Between my playing days and my coaching days, I started an organization called the Leadership Zone and spoke at quite a few leadership seminars.

At one seminar, a woman in the audience was staring at me. The more I talked, the more she frowned and the angrier she became. Finally, at break time I pulled her aside and asked, "Ma'am, what's wrong?"

She glared at me, "I don't like you! You look just like him."

I was stunned. "Like who?"

She snarled, "My brother! When you walked into the room, the way you walked, you had this proud look. You thought you knew everything, and you thought you had all the answers!"

The hurt and pain flowed forth as she continued, "He and I had an argument and he would not say he was sorry. He just would not! And you remind me of him."

I softened. "You miss your brother, don't you?"

She began to sob. Through tears she cried, "Yes!"

I asked, "You want to call him, don't you? How long has it been?"

It had been five years.

"Just call him," I said tenderly. "He misses you, too. You need to call him."

By the end of the day she thought that I was great.

Another woman at the seminar was a lesbian. She said, "I'm a Christian. I read my Bible and pray just like you do. I'm the way I am and you're the way you are, and that's just it. Why can't we just love each other?"

I waited until she was done, then replied.

"Ma'am, I didn't write the Bible. I just decided to build my life on what it says. I don't hate you. I care about you and value you as a human being. I'm not judging you. Just like everyone else, I've got my own issues to deal with. But every day I strive to live as the Bible commands. This is a choice that I have made for myself."

At the end of the day, I don't think that she thought that I was too great. With both women, God allowed me to be a messenger, but I learned something, too.

Then I heard the Lord asking, "Whom should I send as a messenger to my people? Who will go for us?" And I said, "Lord, I'll go! Send me" (Isa. 6:8).

My flight attendant didn't like me. I don't know why. The guy next to me noticed it right away.

I made a special point of saying "thank you" every time she did something for me. I was watching the movie and she told me to take off my headphones because I was saying "thank you" too loudly. I couldn't win.

I had sat next to three people during the course of the day and had talked about God with two of them. The third slept the whole time. United Airlines had Going the Extra Mile coupons that we frequent flyers could give to airline employees who went above and beyond the call of duty. I filled one out and as I disembarked, I gave it to the attendant who did not like me. I didn't do it to heap hot coals on her head; rather, my motive was pure. I genuinely wanted to improve her day. What bothered me most was that she couldn't see Christ in me.

Why couldn't she see Jesus in Jay when two others had? I was filled with the Spirit. I'd done devotions, prayed and even sang about my awesome God. I was ready to minister to anyone God put in my path. The flight attendant was in my path, but resistant.

I'm reminded of those who wanted to throw Jesus off a cliff overlooking Nazareth but couldn't see Him.¹ The flight attendant who didn't like me behaved like she wanted to throw me out of the plane. Perhaps she did see Christ in me after all and didn't like Him.

I guess the bottom line is that only those people who are prepared beforehand by the Holy Spirit of God will see Jesus in any of us. God is preparing people all around us. Our job is to be ready with the right message when God brings along our path someone whom He has prepared.

Are you ready?

Wonderful Designer of Heavenly Appointments, I want to be available for whatever encounter You have in mind, be it friendly or hostile. God, would You fill me with Your Spirit so that those whom You put in my path might see Christ in me? Thank You.

SINGULARITY COMMENTARY

Hard to the Core

I visited a woman's prison in 1996. The chaplain warned me that most of the inmates were hardcore and had been hurt, mostly by men. Husbands and boyfriends were common culprits, but fathers had done most of the damage. Rape, abuse, abandonment and neglect had put these women in an emotional prison without bars. I was warned that although they didn't know me, most would hate me, just because of my gender.

I was the guest speaker at the prison. As I began to talk, it was clear that I wasn't cutting it. My audience was disconnected, disinterested and bored. I had to switch gears. Instead of telling them about Jesus, the Spirit prompted me to show them how much God loved them. I took an unusual step. I stood in as a proxy for all of the men who had ever hurt them. I told the women that they could put all of the blame and pain on me.

I moved closer to them, fell on my knees and began to pray. Even though I was not the one who had actually hurt them, I started by asking for forgiveness: "I'm sorry for what I did. I didn't know how much I would hurt you. I guess I didn't care. But, I want you to know that from the bottom of my heart, I'm really, really sorry. Will you forgive me? I know you want to hurt me and spit on me, but I'm asking you instead to accept my apology and forgive me. Put it on me and look toward God. He sent me here to tell you that today you have a choice to make. Will you forgive me? Will you accept your freedom?"

As I prayed, tears flooded from nearly every eye in the room. I was crying, too. I remained on my knees as the women came forward to pray and to hug me. It was a powerful moment that I will never forget. I was tuned in to the Spirit and God did a mighty work that day.

But when the Holy Spirit has come upon you, you will receive power and will tell people about me everywhere—in Jerusalem, throughout Judea, in Samaria, and to the ends of the earth (Acts 1:8).

Paul was in jail again, this time with Silas. Their accusers had stripped them bare, beaten them with sticks, shackled their ankles and thrown them into a rat- and roach-infested hardcore hellhole. Instead of whining and sniveling about how bad it was, Paul and Silas listened to God's Spirit and began preaching, singing and praising God. They saw opportunity in the midst of harrowing circumstances.

Paul later wrote, "Dear brothers and sisters, whenever trouble comes your way, let it be an opportunity for joy. For when your faith is tested, your endurance has a chance to grow."[1] The apostle had learned to listen to and rely upon the Holy Spirit.

After what were probably hours of praise, God let Paul know it was Spirit time. A strong earthquake hit, opening all of the cell doors in the prison and loosing all the prisoners' chains. That wasn't even the main miracle—there was more coming.

Upon discovering the open doors, the jailer started to kill himself. In those days, jailers literally put their lives on the line. If a prisoner escaped, the jailer would be publicly tortured and killed. He drew his sword and readied himself to commit suicide when he heard Paul's shout, "Don't do it. We are all here!"[2]

Paul could have left. Everyone could have run. But instead, Paul listened to God's Spirit and stayed. Following Paul's lead, none of the inmates made a break for it; even the most hardened of criminals stayed. To the jailer's surprise, they had all gone into Paul's cell.

Paul waited for God to do something great. We don't know how many prisoners listened to his message. Since no one left, probably all of them received Christ as savior. We do know that the jailer gave himself to the Lord and immediately took Paul and Silas to his home to get his household saved, too. God worked a miracle that night.

It's amazing what can happen when we remain available, listen to the Holy Spirit and obey. Just amazing.

Great God of Miracles, teach me to wait upon You and listen intently to Your quiet voice. Show me how to turn down the volume of the world and turn up Your speech. Then give me the courage to go to my core, so that I can curtail my flesh and wait upon Your miraculous works. Here I am God, use me. Thank You.

TODAY'S READING: ACTS 1:6-11; 2:22-42; 16:19-34; ROMANS 8:1-11; 1 CORINTHIANS 2:6—3:9; EPHESIANS 5:18-21

Joy to the World

Kim and I missed celebrating Christmas with the kids in 1999. If our military troops had to give up the holidays with their families, we could sacrifice, too. We went on a USO tour that included stops at military bases in Kosovo.

I'm very patriotic. I stand at attention when a flag passes by me. I love my country. And I am deeply grateful to men and women who put themselves in harm's way for the cause of freedom. It was an honor to give something back to those who were giving so much.

Each person did his or her thing. Terry Bradshaw and Al Franken were funny. Christie Brinkley and the Dallas Cowboy Cheerleaders were beautiful. Ruth Pointer of the Pointer Sisters, Mary Chapin Carpenter and Shane Minor sang songs. John Glenn and I talked.

As profound as the time with the troops was, another memorable event occurred during the airplane ride home. We were all exhausted from the grueling trip and mellow because it was Christmastime. We thought about our loved ones back home and started singing Christmas songs. It was almost magical to be caught up in the moment as we blended our voices—some were professionals and others were not. No one was singing to impress anyone else; rather, we simply lifted our voices and were filled with joy.

On the trip, we had become family. Back home we all had myriad issues—kids, marriages, finances, health and who knows what else. On that airplane ride, all differences and problems disappeared. We had come together from different walks of life to share a common cause to do something profoundly good halfway around the world for those who were risking their lives for us. We had given what we could and now we sang for joy as we winged our way home.

I don't believe a person has to know the Lord to experience the joy of the Lord. All good things are from God, and this was definitely a good thing.

I am overwhelmed with joy in the LORD my God! (Isa. 61:10).

Joy is one of the primary themes of the Bible. There are 323 references to the concept.[1] By contrast, the word "love" is used 312 times, "peace" 332 times and the combined usage of "saved" and "salvation" total 245 times.[2] Apparently joy is a very big deal to God.

Biblically, joy is defined as "the happy state that results from knowing and serving God."[3] Even a secular definition includes a spiritual reference. Joy is the "feeling of great happiness or pleasure, especially of an elevated or spiritual kind."[4]

The English word for hedonism comes from the Greek word for pleasure. Although there is nothing wrong with pleasure, it can become addictive. In fact, it frequently becomes self-centered to the point of becoming sin.[5] Also, it is clear that the self-indulgent pursuit of pleasure never results in joy or fulfillment.[6] Biblical joy is never guilty of such consequences. In fact, the Bible separates pleasure from joy. In other words, too much pleasure is bad for us, but we can never experience too much joy.

We should not make the mistake of always relating happiness to joy. There are times when we won't be happy, but we can still be filled with joy. A woman going through labor isn't having a good time. She isn't happy that she is feeling pain, but she is joyful as she anticipates the birth of a child.[7] Jesus wasn't happy being scourged and hung on a cross to die, but He was joyful about doing His Father's will.[8] Mike and Kim weren't happy being away from their kids at Christmas time, but they too rejoiced in doing what God wanted.

God has plans for each of us.[9] His ultimate plan is that we might find Him through Jesus Christ. The purpose of creation can only be fulfilled in our salvation, so nothing brings God greater joy than a soul saved.[10] Similarly, we can know no greater joy than to find God and walk uprightly with Him.[11]

God created joy and He wants us to be joyful, even at 36,000 feet.

Dear Author of Joy, I want to walk with You, be filled with Your Spirit and experience Your joy. Guard me from being self-indulgent, forgive me for being selfish and fill me with Your Spirit. I want to know the joy of the Lord. Thank You.

TODAY'S READING: NEHEMIAH 8:10-12; LUKE 15:3-10; JOHN 16:1-24; HEBREWS 12:1-2; PHILIPPIANS 4:4-7

Surprise

One night, Kim and I had a fight. We argued and after a while I decided I was going to win. It had gone beyond anyone making a point, and what we were arguing about did not matter. I was standing up as the man of the house, insisting that I knew what I was talking about. She knew what to do when I got that way. She went to bed.

While I wanted to be the "man of the house," I wanted even more to be a man of God. I knew that even though I had won the argument, I had lost. Licking my wounds, I opened the Bible and read. The Lord led me to what is called the "Love Chapter," in 1 Corinthians 13. I read and reread all 13 verses—for more than three hours! At 2 A.M., I finally got it.

God showed me that I didn't know anything about love. Everything that I thought I had known about love was what I'd seen in others, and that wasn't much. I needed to learn how to love at a new level, with purity. My love needed to be unconditional and patient. It wasn't.

God's love heals; mine hurt. His love succeeds; mine failed. His love shows mercy; mine demanded. I'd never really loved with God's kind of love—not from the deepest part of my being and not to the fullest extent. God made it clear that I had to love with a love that asks for forgiveness. I had to go to Kim and say, "I'm sorry."

For the first time, I realized that I had never loved Kim with this type of love. I ran upstairs and woke her up at two in the morning. My intentions were great, but my timing was terrible. Pointing to the Love Chapter, I said, "Read this! You've got to read this."

Rubbing her sleepy eyes she said, "You read it. It's two o'clock in the morning."

I read the chapter out loud and promised, "Kim, from this day on, the love that I show to you will be this kind of love."

I pray that your hearts will be flooded with light so that you can understand the wonderful future he has promised to those he called. I want you to realize what a rich and glorious inheritance he has given to his people. I pray that you will begin to understand the incredible greatness of his power for us who believe him (Eph. 1:18-19).

Twenty-two years ago a dear friend got in my face: "Jay, I think God's got a chance of using you, but you'd better get your marriage together."

I was shocked.

"What? I've got a good marriage!"

He smiled but cut deeply, "Sometimes you speak to your wife harshly. Do you have any unfulfilled expectations or do you resent the compromises you've made?"

I was uncomfortable.

"Back off a little. We're doing fine."

He continued, "You have to find out what it means to be a 'crucified husband.' Learn to die for your wife as Christ died for the church."

That's when a light went on inside my head. It was an epiphany. I like to call it an ah-ha experience. God wanted me to learn about this "crucified" concept and then do it.

I told my wife, Mary, about the conversation and that I'd decided to be a crucified husband. I thought she'd say, "Oh honey, that's so wonderful." And I figured there would be gestures of gratitude.

It didn't go down that way. She said, "Show me! I'm tired of all the talk."

There would be no immediate payoff. I was left with changing my outlook and my behavior simply because God said to do it.

As of this writing, Mary and I have been married for more than 40 years. I've thought about writing a book on marriage and I asked Mary what she thought about it. "Not yet," she replied, "But you're getting closer."

I continue to be a work in progress.

An epiphanic experience is a lasting intuitive leap of understanding from God. It's an event that we never forget. It is a turning point at which we say, "Ah-ha! Now I get it." God getting through to our head is the first step. Us putting His words into action is the next. When that happens I like to think that God says, "Ah-ha! Now you've got it."

Great God of Surprises and Revelations, thank You for the obvious times when You have spoken to me with words, thoughts and understanding. Remind me when I stop pursuing Your leading. Get my attention when I wander. Give me the desire to be diligent about continuing to do Your will. Thank You. Amen.

TODAY'S READING: PSALM 25:12-15; 1 CORINTHIANS 13:1-13; EPHESIANS 1:3-23; 5:25-33

Father and Son

My parents got a divorce when I was a kid. I sided with my mom, refused to forgive my dad and didn't talk with him for many years.

Mostly I was able to quash thoughts of reconciliation, but God finally made it clear that I had to act. I had been speaking in prisons, encouraging the inmates to reconcile with their fathers, but that was hypocritical because I had a dad to whom I wouldn't speak.

Kim called me on it: "Mike, how can you tell other people to reconcile with their loved ones when you won't call your dad? Are you going to forgive him or is the blood of Jesus going to be in vain?"

Mending my relationship with my father was for me, but it was also for the children whom, at the time, I had not yet had (I now have seven!). Sin is generational. The sins of the father are passed along. I wanted to come clean and start a new generation with love and forgiveness, so I made the call. I needed to ask my dad to forgive me. I also needed to forgive him, too. And I needed to ask God to forgive me for my hatred toward my father.

My dad and talked on the phone for three hours. To say it was emotional is an understatement. There was some screaming and some crying—each one of us almost hung up several times, but we stayed with it. By the end of our talk, God had done a wonderful work. I forgave my dad, he forgave me and we started a new relationship.

A couple of months later, I visited my dad. We hugged each other, and for the first time in my life, I told him that I loved him. I listened as he told me about how he grew up, and I began to understand the dynamics that shaped the man he had become.

As I write this book, my father's health is failing. He is now bedridden. It was good for both of us to get our relationship right and enjoy each other while we could.

The son said to him, "Father, I have sinned against heaven and against you; I am no longer worthy to be called your son" (Luke 15:21, *NIV*).

The young man couldn't call. There were no phones. He couldn't send a message. He had no money. Actually, it is not clear whether he would have if he could have. He was ashamed.

He had dreamed about the good life, had talked his dad into giving him his inheritance and had left the farm to the farmers. Kicking the manure off his feet, he left for the city without looking back. The dad had watched his son walk out of sight. It was dark before the father gave up his gaze, only to resume his post the next day—and the next and the next.

The young man left the animals on the farm and became a party animal himself. However, after a ride in the fast lane, he found that the pigs had it better than he did. He squandered his money and lived on the street. The so-called good life had ruined the farmer's boy.

The lad was filthy, penniless and starving. He may have thought about suicide but chose to eat crow. He wondered whether his father would let him come back and decided to find out. Ashamed and embarrassed, the prodigal headed home, hoping his dad would take him back as a hired hand, rehearsing his confession as he walked.

The dad still stood at his post and was the first to see his son returning. The old man's heart almost jumped out of his chest as he ran to hug and kiss his boy.

The young rebel was broken: "Father, I have sinned against both heaven and you, and I am no longer worthy of being called your son."[1]

Confession is the first step to forgiveness and reconciliation, but there is a risk in taking that step. Neither Mike nor the young man knew if their father would forgive them and reconcile. Unlike reconciliation with an earthly father, we don't have to worry about the risk with our Heavenly Father. We can tell Him we're sorry we went away. He'll forgive us and welcome us back every time. In fact, He is waiting at His post right now.

Forgiving Father, I confess my sins to You. I have wandered away.
Thank You for welcoming me back. Lord, show me the people I have
wronged along the way and give me the courage to make calls of confession.
I pray for reconciliation, but if it's not possible, I thank You that no
matter what happens in this world, I am reconciled with You.

TODAY'S READING: LUKE 15:1-32; ROMANS 8:12-17; GALATIANS 3:23—4:7

Goodbye, Mom

I was 5 years old when one of my brothers died. I was too young to process it. I was 12 when another brother passed away. There was more loss for me with him because he had helped raise me after my dad left. Another brother died in 2005. That was hard in a different way. We had been through so many years together.

My mom passed away in 2004. She was 82. I knew things weren't quite right with her health and the Lord began to prepare me in the last few weeks of her life. But it was still unexpected because she was my mom.

For a long time, Mom was everything to me. She suffered so much in life. I prayed, *Lord, if You're going to take my mom, would You let it be quick so she doesn't have to suffer anymore?* She had had a long, tough life.

When my sister first called to tell me that Mom fell and they were trying to find a pulse, I grabbed my Bible and went outside. I began to pray, "Lord, don't take her, don't take her. Let me talk to her, let me speak to her again. Let me hold her—." Then I was reminded of what I had asked God just a few weeks before. God honored my prayer. He took her quickly. No suffering. No pain.

God went a step further. He also gave me a vision. I didn't see it with my eyes, but I saw it in my spirit. God spoke to my spirit: *Do you really want me to bring her back? Look!* At that moment I could see my mom running, jumping and shouting for joy. I know it sounds strange, but it was as real as sitting at Starbucks with a friend. I saw her having a blast when God asked, "Do you really want Me to bring her back?"

I said, "No, Lord. I don't." I miss her a lot, but I let her go.

For we know that when this earthly tent we live in is taken down—when we die and leave these bodies—we will have a home in heaven, an eternal body made for us by God himself and not by human hands (2 Cor. 5:1).

We have all lost loved ones. It's a difficult part of life.

I have several friends who have lost a child. Frankly, I can't imagine the pain and the sense of loss. It's a devastating event. It happened twice to Mike's mom.

Thankfully, I haven't experienced that kind of loss, but my mom, dad and a step-mom, with whom I was very close, have all died. Each loss was difficult.

As I noted in *Coach Wooden One-on-One*, my mother had a hard life and made many bad choices. There was a time when she was a skid-row alcoholic who gave her body away at night for a place to stay. The Lord allowed me to lead her to Christ when she was 64 years old. She died three years later. She was living in Southern California. I was living in Oregon when I got the news. I preached at her funeral. I was sad, but there was also a sense of relief. She was in the Kingdom, and for me some of the pain of being an adult child of an alcoholic was over.

I led my dad to Christ three weeks before he died and I led my step-mom to the Lord 18 months before she died. Both passed away within 13 months of each other, in the same hospice facility, with me holding a hand and praying.

To have been able to lead all three to the Savior is an unspeakable gift from God for which I will be eternally grateful. I am not a sufficient enough wordsmith to communicate my gratitude to my Lord for allowing me the privilege. I'm looking forward to conversations with my parents without having the family baggage hanging over our heads. I miss them, but I could let them all go because I knew where they were going.

If given the opportunity, do you know how to lead your loved ones to the Lord? Are you praying daily for their salvation?

Dear Author of Salvation, thank You for Jesus Christ and for saving me. Prepare me to tell others about You and answer my prayers on behalf of my loved ones. Lead them to Yourself and save their souls. I'll be happy to be Your agent, but it's okay if I'm not. I just want to know they are OK. Thank You. Amen.

A Real Man

Raising children who have principles and character takes preparation and work, but it's what a parent is supposed to do. That's why I have been intentional about being a dad.

I want to instill values in my children's minds when they are young so that when they grow older those values will have a better chance of settling into their hearts. I want my sons to grow up to be what I call real men and I want my daughters to become real women. Periodically we talk about it.

A few years ago, when my son, Matthew, was 12, I asked him to tell me what it takes to be a real man. He said he wasn't sure, but I knew he knew something about it because we had talked about it a few weeks prior. However, I wasn't sure how much he'd remember.

I asked him to think about it and then try to define it. He got the first characteristic right when he said, "A real man loves his family."

I urged him to continue, "What else?" He knew there was more, but it was slow coming back to him.

He told me he didn't know, but I didn't let him off the hook. I wanted him to think. "Come on now, what else makes a real man?"

I could tell the gears were turning in his head and it was fun to see when the lights came on. He was excited when he said, "A real man keeps his word and obeys God." He pursed his lips and pondered the question. Then it came out. "And a real man is a hard worker," he blurted, with a big smile.

Matthew is now dealing with some of the questions of manhood. The truth is in his mind. My wife, Kim, and I made sure that he knows what makes up a real man. Our prayer is that those truths have sunk in and he becomes one. I know that he is well on his way.

But you, Timothy, belong to God; so run from all these evil things, and follow what is right and good. Pursue a godly life, along with faith, love, perseverance, and gentleness (1 Tim. 6:11).

The apostle Paul was a real man. He endured shipwrecks, beatings, a stoning—the list of headaches and tough turns is long. Paul came through it all and glorified God as he did so.

Paul had values and was ready to pass them along, but he most likely never married nor did he have children of his own that we know about. Timothy was like a son to Paul, but still not his own. Paul called Timothy, "My beloved and trustworthy child in the Lord."[1]

We assume that the apostle led Timothy to the Lord during Paul's first missionary journey. On his second missionary journey, Paul added Timothy to his entourage after John Mark got cold feet and left. It made sense, because by that time Timothy was a well-respected man.[2] Paul discipled Timothy and dispatched him on many crucial missions.[3] Near the end of Paul's life, Paul wanted Timothy by his side.[4]

Where Mike was intentional about being a father, the apostle Paul was intentional about being a discipler. God had told Paul that He only wanted real men to be in charge in His Church. Paul wrote out God's list of characteristics that make up a real man and sent it to Timothy. The list was long.

A real man must be a person whose life cannot be spoken against. He must be faithful to his wife. He must exhibit self-control, live wisely, and have a good reputation. He must enjoy having guests in his home and must be able to teach. He must not be a heavy drinker or be violent. He must be gentle, peace loving, and not one who loves money. He must manage his own family well, with children who respect and obey him. He must not be a new Christian, because he might be proud of being chosen so soon. Also, people outside the church must speak well of him.[5]

Timothy was older than Matthew Singletary, so God's list was longer than Mike's. Nonetheless, both our heavenly father and earthly dads everywhere want their sons to become real men.

If you're a son, God's list is for you, too.

Heavenly Father, I aspire to the highest calling for my life that fits in with Your perfect plans. I don't want anything in my life to get in the way of Your call. Oh God, mold me into a real man. I want the list in my heart to be reflected in my life. Thank You. (If you are a female, pray that the males in your life might acquire the nature of real men.)

TODAY'S READING: 1 TIMOTHY 3:1-12; 6:3-16

Memories. Mike and Grant Teaff talk about their Baylor days (left). In 2001, Mike sang "Take Me Out to the Ball Game" at Chicago's Wrigley Field (below).

The Singletarys. Mike and Kim's oldest daughter, Kristen, graduated from high school in 2005 (below). There will be many more graduations to come. The Singletary children (above): Matt, Kristen and Jill (top row); Brooke, John, Becky and Jackie (bottom row)

Back in the Game

I got teary-eyed my first game back. It had been 10 years since I'd been on the grass on game day. I walked out on the field as a Ravens coach and was overwhelmed. Standing there on the sidelines, I remembered how much I love the game.

It felt great to be back, but I didn't catch myself wishing I could play again. Rather, I caught myself being grateful to God. Silently I prayed, *Lord, I am so thankful to You for saving me from coaching this game earlier. I know that I couldn't have handled it any earlier.*

I am truly thankful every day that I coach. I am glad to be around the game, but it has changed. The salaries have escalated, and that has changed the relationship between the players and the coaches. The coaches don't have very much authority anymore. The owners have changed, too. They want to win right away. A new head coach only has three years to turn a program around. Sometimes he only has two. Owners want victory *now*.

As a result of this heightened stress, player development is skimped and coaches seek out players who can deliver results right away. This can be counterproductive. To put pressure on rookies is like telling the coach to turn a 14-year-old boy into a man in two or three years. Soccer players, tennis players and gymnasts mature early, but it doesn't happen in football.

As a linebacker coach, I get my guys for 10 to 12 minutes a day. The rest of the time we do things as a team or break off into special team units. That isn't much time for me to train them—I always feel rushed. I pray, *Lord, how am I going to help these kids with only the few minutes a day that I have. What can I do to make the most of the time that I have with them? Give me the wisdom. Give me the discernment to help these kids not only become better football players but also become better men.*

Even though the game has changed, my commitment to the players hasn't.

Jesus replied, " 'You must love the Lord your God with all your heart, all your soul, and all your mind.' This is the first and greatest commandment. A second is equally important: 'Love your neighbor as yourself.' All the other commandments and all the demands of the prophets are based on these two commandments" (Matt. 22:37-40).

By asking God for discernment in how to best use a limited amount of time, Mike is trying to boil football down to its essentials—what can be called non-negotiables. Let's look at the Christian faith through a similar lens. What are its non-negotiables?

People who attend traditional churches want old hymns sung out of hymnbooks, not praise choruses flashed on the wall. Liturgical churches want members to dress up a bit for formal worship, experience bells, smells, rituals and reverential silence. Casual churches don't care how attendees look and usually rock out a bit with their music. Pentecostals put extra emphasis on spiritual gifts and worship. Conservatives accentuate the Bible. Evangelicals put more umph in evangelism. Mennonites want justice for everyone. Moderates are into social action. Emergents promote community and question everything traditional.

Who is right?

Most issues aren't non-negotiables. They're peripheral.

I had a wart on my hand. The doctor took it off. I don't miss it. It was a peripheral issue. I am a Christian. If I were sent to Tibet and told that I had to follow the Dalai Lama, I would have to resist, fake it or irreversibly change the heart of who I am. A wart is negotiable. What lies at the core of our being should not be a negotiable.

Beyond believing in Jesus as Savior, what are the other non-negotiatiables of our faith?

Jesus told us to love God and love people in the same way that we love ourselves. While there are some other details, when our heart's first priority is to love others, most everything else takes care of itself.[1] We need to love widows, orphans, the poor, the sick, the afflicted and prisoners—for Christ's sake. When loving others is at our core, it will not matter how much the world changes; we will still want to be in the game, telling others about Jesus.

Wonderful God of Love, I want to love You like You love me. I know that's impossible, but it is the desire of my heart. And I would also like to learn to love people in the same way that You love them. I desire to love You enough to stay pure and love people enough to show concern in every way. Father, make these things happen in my life. Thank You.

TODAY'S READING: MATTHEW 22:37-40; 28:19-20; JOHN 13:34-35; JAMES 1:19-27; 1 JOHN 4:20-21

Eye to Eye

Money, possessions, sex and fame are all part of the world of professional football. For the most part, all that these idols do is turn kids into older kids. The kids get older but they don't grow up. They don't think, talk or act like men. Football players, no matter their age, need good role models and good teachers.

I have had some good teachers. The best ones held me accountable. They'd start by asking, "Mike, do you understand this?"

"Yes, I understand it," I'd say, even if I didn't, because my friends were watching.

"OK," my teachers would say, "Since you understand, go to the chalkboard and show us."

The board is where the rubber would meet the road. When I had to go to that board, in front of my peers, I would sweat and the cockiness would slink away. Sometimes I would stutter.

Marker boards are good tools. I use them now that I am a teacher.

I ask my linebackers if they understand my point. When they say yes, I send them to the board. I say, "When you go to the board, you need to look us in the eyes. You need to express yourself. You need to be sure of yourself. I want you to teach me."

I require my charges to look me in the eye and say, "Yes, Sir," or "No, Sir." I don't allow them to be looking around the room. They have to stand up like men. Giving them respect in return gives me the right to talk to them about how to handle money, stay out of trouble and not let fame go to their heads.

One player said, "Coach, I appreciate you telling me this. I never had a dad. I never had a man around me. I just didn't know."

I know God has called me to help make men of boys. I will do that as I coach. I will strive every day to show them a picture of what a godly man looks like. I will look them eye-to-eye and do all that I can—with God's help—to be that picture.

So, my dear friends, flee from the worship of idols (1 Cor. 10:14).

The idols we worship have ownership of our hearts. When we have a divided heart, we aren't rational. That's true today and it was true back when worshiping Dagon was the rage.[1]

The Philistines had captured the Ark of God and had taken it into the temple of their god, Dagon. The next day the statue of Dagon was found before the Ark, face down in a posture of worship.

Phil the Philistine propped up the idol, but at sunup the following day, he again found Dagon down. This time its head and hands had been severed.

God brought His judgment on the area around the Philistine temple in the form of devastation, affliction, panic, an outbreak of tumors and death. (Some old English biblical translations render the Hebrew word for tumor as "hemorrhoid."[2] Can you imagine hemorrhoids so bad that people didn't just walk funny, but also thousands died? What I wouldn't give to have had the corner on the Preparation H market during those times!

The people realized that all of their problems were consequences of stealing God's box—the Ark. The Philistines knew that the God of the Jews was supreme and that He had authority over Dagon. And they acknowledged judgment was coming. Word traveled fast. Two entire towns refused to house the Ark after they heard about the hemorrhoid outbreak.[3]

I would have thought that a plague of hemmies would be enough to change the people's allegiance. Let me think: hemorrhoids or blessings, which would I prefer? It's a no-brainer—unless you are a Philistine.

These people refused to transfer their worship from their god to the Jewish God. They stuck with Dagon. Why? With Dagon the people wouldn't have to change. On the other hand, the God of the Jews demanded holiness.

Not much has changed. Money, possessions, sex and fame are powerful idols. They'll take over a person's heart. A few of Mike's guys will listen, choose to follow the Lord and grow up to become real men. But many won't.

How about you? Will you let go of your idols and turn to God? Or will you be a Dagon dummy?

Father in Heaven, You are the one true God. You rule and reign in heaven and on Earth. Lord, keep me from choosing substitutes for You. There are no gods like You. I want to turn from all idols and worship You alone. Amen.

TODAY'S READING: 1 SAMUEL 5:1-12; 1 CORINTHIANS 10:14-22; 1 PETER 3:13-4:6

The Team

When building a team, most head coaches start with a quarterback. I am different. When I become a head coach, I'll start by hiring a great staff. I'll look for flexible men who aren't afraid to think outside the box. I'll want them to love the game but to love the players even more. They'll have to be men of character, men with strong morals—including honesty and trustworthiness. I'll want my team to reflect these qualities, so my coaches will have to emulate these values, too. I want to know that when we go into battle, these men aren't going to run.

NFL games are almost always decided in the trenches, so my first player priorities will be linemen, both offensive and defensive. If a team owns the line of scrimmage, it always has a chance to win.

Next, I will find a quarterback. He won't have to have a great arm, and he won't have to be a rocket scientist. I will want a quarterback who will look me in the eyes when we're losing—whose expression will tell me that he still believes he can win. He'll be a leader who will make the team better because he never gives up.

We'll work with the backs and receivers. We only need one who can run, and we'll look for an outside man who is fast and always a threat deep. We'll need someone who is willing to go over the middle and can catch a three- to five-yard pass.

On the defensive side, I'll look for a linebacker who's smart and a leader. I will also want a safety, particularly a weak safety, who's very smart, knows where the ball is going, and can anticipate the opposition's next move. I'll want my special teams to be disciplined. That's my football team.

If the Lord wills and I get the call to be a head coach, I'll dismiss the existing coaches who don't fit and I'll trade the players who don't buy into what I want to do. At first, the town might not like the changes, but they will when we win.

But God made our bodies with many parts, and he has put each part just where he wants it (1 Cor. 12:18).

If I wanted to win in the NBA, I'd coach one of the elite teams. God would go with the worst team. If I were picking countries to be on my side during a war, I'd start with the United States. God would go with tiny, little Israel. To win a brain buster contest, I'd go with a high-IQ crowd. God would go with a Down Syndrome kid.

If I wanted to change the world, I'd go with the richest person (Bill Gates) or the most powerful (the president of the United States). Not God! He uses Mother Teresa types. I can only think of one person who got more done with less. Jesus.

Christ was born in a stable in an insignificant town. His folks had to take him to a foreign country to keep him from being killed. He never owned anything and had to mooch everything, including all of his food, a donkey for a ride and the use of an upper room. But without the benefit of CNN or Fox News, He changed the world. Time is marked by His presence on Earth, and through Him our salvation is assured.

I would have done it with life. God did it all through death—the death of a dirt poor, thirty-three-year-old guy who didn't have a dime and didn't own a pencil. Our Father operates in very strange ways. Obviously, His criteria for building a team are different from mine.

Jesus did it the same way. The Son's team was a bunch of rag-tag misfits. How He ever thought He could change the world with Peter, John and the rest is beyond me. But He did.

I guess this means that there is hope for us. We're not Bill Gates or the president. In the grand scheme of things, we're rather inconsequential. That makes us perfect candidates for God's use. His specialty is doing great things with the most ordinary people He can find.

There is one catch. We have to be willing to fill our role on God's team. I am willing. Are you?

Dear Lord, I love being on Your team. Thank You for choosing me. Show me my position. I want to play it with all my heart for Your honor and glory. I am humbled when I think that You want to use me to do great things. Thank You. Amen.

TODAY'S READING: PSALMS 40:6-8; 105:36—106:3; 119:161-168; ISAIAH 6:8; JOHN 15:13-19; 1 CORINTHIANS 12:12-31; 1 PETER 5:1-5

Little Gun, Big Run

A few years ago, I was asked to be the head coach of my son's junior high team. I declined the top position but offered to be offensive coordinator. My son was slated to be the quarterback. I wanted to be the offensive coordinator because I felt that most offenses were much too complex. Complexities cause players to think when they should be playing fast.

When I'm a head coach, we'll have around 20 plays with many variations. Any one who learns these 20 plays can play on my offensive unit. I believe Vince Lombardi understood the nugget of "well-executed simplicity." That's how I'll coach.

Most coaches are concerned about what the other team knows about them. I don't really care. I want strong enough personnel that we can always run the football. I'm going to run it, run it and run it some more—and toss an occasional deep pass for balance. The question will be, Can the other team stop our run? If I know what I'm doing and my team is flawless in its execution, then it does not matter if the opposition knows the next play call.

Running the football reduces a team's dependency on key players. It doesn't hurt as much if the quarterback goes down, and it allows you to control the clock.

I want my quarterback to be a disciplined leader. I don't need him to win the game. We'll have 11 people and together we will win. The quarterback has to be the kind of guy who won't hurt us.

My team will work hard to prevent turning the ball over. We'll practice to create turnovers by the other team, but I won't be playing guys who turn it over or lose focus. We'll stop the big play and we'll concentrate on special teams. My team will run the ball, make very few fumbles, manage the clock and execute plays with precision. This will be my signature.

Therefore, since we are surrounded by such a huge crowd of witnesses to the life of faith, let us strip off every weight that slows us down, especially the sin that so easily hinders our progress. And let us run with endurance the race that God has set before us (Heb. 12:1).

Players on Mike Singletary's team will not have to be the smartest or the most athletic. However, if they are going to see much action, they will need to know the fundamentals and be disciplined.

Living a successful Christian life is similar. We need to submit to the disciplines of our faith. We should construct a well-disciplined biblical plan and be consistent in fulfilling the plan. If we take these steps, we will ultimately lead successful lives.

We are not required to live spectacular lives, but we are called upon to "run with endurance."[1] This means that we must hang in there. We do not need to attempt great feats for God. We only need to lead righteous lives and consistently apply the basic principles, specifically obedience and perseverance.

At times, being a Christian will be full-tilt exciting. However, we do not generate this excitement; God does. We just say, "Yes, Lord," and tag along for the ride, which can sometimes be a roller coaster. It's really that simple. But simple doesn't mean easy.

Discipline comes from the Latin word "disco." It has nothing to do with John Travolta or the '70s dance craze; rather, it means "to learn" or "get to know something or someone."[2] It refers to the process of learning a way of life.

A disciple is an apprentice who absorbs lessons from a master. The master has learned the discipline and he passes it on to his disciple until the learner can imitate or live like the master. Such learning requires a relationship. To be like Jesus, we must have a relationship with Him.

Do you want to live a successful Christian life? Submit to the disciplines of God.

Great God of Enduring Patience, thank You for being patient with me. I want to learn Your disciplines and be consistent in applying them to my life. Thank You for enduring with me as I learn to run with endurance. I desire to say yes to You in all things and in every area of my life. Amen.

TODAY'S READING: DEUTERONOMY 11:1-12; ISAIAH 14:12-15; HEBREWS 12:1-13

A Winning Strategy

I've been asked what I think are the most crucial elements in a football game. The obvious answer is the score! Beyond that, there are no easy answers.

In one sense, the most crucial part of a game is the play that is about to be run. I know that sounds flippant, but unless the game is a blowout, each play becomes progressively more and more important. This means that each play a team is about to run is more crucial than the previous play. If the score is close, toward the end of the game any big play can be the game breaker.

Controlling the line of scrimmage is the most important aspect of football. The trenches are where the game is won or lost. Owning the line is crucial to consistency.

Winning always revolves around stopping the run. If a team can stop the run, it can then disrupt the opponent's passing game. But if the opponent is running at will, they can also pass at will. Clearly, controlling the line of scrimmage and stopping the run are interrelated.

The next issue involves big plays and turnovers. A team doesn't have to make big plays, but it does have to eliminate them from being made by an opponent. A team that turns the ball over more than its opponent does cannot consistently win. If a team can't stop the big play, or if it keeps turning over the ball, controlling the line of scrimmage won't save it.

Let's look at the defense. A team needs to be able to stop the run and stop big plays and turnovers. Period! Ideally, on offense, a team wants to control the football, preferably with short runs and short passes. Teams should only go down the field occasionally, just to keep the game honest.

If I'm a head coach, I'll have an offense that's always moving. I will not come out of the huddle and have the same look on each play. The opposition will never know exactly what's coming. I may not line up in the same formation during a series. We'll keep the defense guessing. That is how I will coach and how my team will win.

Then he asked them, "Who do you say I am?" Peter replied, "You are the Messiah sent from God!" (Luke 9:20).

Jesus had a winning strategy—and it started with a crucial question. He asked His disciples, "But who do you say that I am?"

The word "you" in the question is personal and emphatic. Jesus wasn't asking for a report or for information, nor was He interested in what the crowds really thought. Jesus demanded a personal response from His guys. Peter had the right answer: "You are the Messiah sent from God!"[1]

Peter's answer didn't save him. Knowing about Christ doesn't solve the problem of separation from God. The demons know Jesus is the Messiah, but the knowledge doesn't make them born again.[2] So, saying the right words isn't proof of a personal relationship with Jesus. The crucial connection is the heart.

Why should God let a person into heaven? Most people respond, "Because I am a good person." But, that's the wrong answer. How good is good? Compared to Hitler we're not so bad, but compared to Christ we're not very good at all. Relative responses won't cut it.

Actually, when we are dead and standing before God we won't have a thing to say. We'll be stone-silent speechless.[3] Since there won't be an opportunity to say anything, our response to life's most crucial question must be given while we're alive.

What do you believe? Is Jesus your Lord? Is He showing up in your life more and more? Is there evidence of Him at work in how you think and what you do? Is Jesus making a difference? Jesus as Lord in your life is the crucial element of a successful faith. His working is your confirmation. If you are looking more and more like Jesus, your life has answered the crucial question. What do you see when you look in a mirror? When it comes to eternity, what is your winning strategy?

Dear Lord of Heaven and Earth, I want You to be the Lord of my life. I want You to rule and reign in me. I want every nook and cranny of my being to be illuminated by the light of my Lord Jesus Christ. Take over, Father. I don't want to get in Your way. Thank You. Amen.

TODAY'S READING: LUKE 9:20; ACTS 11:19-26; ROMANS 3:10-20

The Machine

As a linebacker coach, I get 10 to 12 minutes alone with my guys during a two-hour practice. That's it. The rest of the time they are running with other groups or doing team drills and scrimmages. I have to maximize the minutes I have.

It's difficult to keep players engaged and in a mode of constant improvement. It's so easy to let a regimen become mundane. As coach, I have to avoid this trap because players won't get better when they're bored.

One thing I did to maximize my coaching time was to create a machine. The Lord gave me the vision and showed me how to put it together. The result is magnificent.

The machine teaches players how to hit, keeping them in a low position. When they hit the machine, an object pops out and they hit it as quickly as they can. Then they go on to the next object. It's like a car wash. It's an all-in-one assembly line. Everything linebackers need to improve upon happens at the machine, so we've eliminated a lot of wasted time. We don't have to run to different places on the field. It all happens on the machine.

When I first brought my machine to the field, most of the coaches looked at it and laughed; but they're not laughing now. After watching us use it, the Ravens' defensive coordinator said, "Mike, I want to tell you. That machine is fantastic!"

The machine has certainly helped me get the most out of my coaching minutes.

This is the new, life-giving way that Christ has opened up for us through the sacred curtain, by means of his death for us (Heb. 10:20).

Mike's machine is where physical work happens, just as the Tabernacle in the Old Testament was where spiritual work happened. The Tabernacle was where life's issues were addressed. It was the place where the people of Israel went to meet God and allow Him to provide for their spiritual growth.[1]

The Tabernacle was placed in the center of the camp so that everyone could see it. As a way to let the people know that God was present, the pillar of cloud by day and the pillar of fire by night rested over the Tabernacle, unless the camp was on the move.

God chose the finest artists to design the Tabernacle and the best materials for its construction. Taking seven months to craft,[2] it was made of 2,200 pounds of gold, 7,543 pounds of silver and 5,310 pounds of bronze.[3] God's instructions were intricate. This was the Father's house, and He wanted it built right.

The Tabernacle was the place where the people exercised their spirituality.[4] It was a house of sacrifice, the site where sin was atoned. Priests came there to represent the people to God and God to the people.

The death of Jesus Christ changed the role of the Tabernacle. At the moment of His death, the curtain that separated the Holy of Holies (the center spot where God was present) in the Tabernacle from the rest of the tent was split from top to bottom. From that moment forward, it was no longer necessary to have a priest take the sins of the people to God. With the death of Christ, everyone gained equal access to the Father. Individuals no longer needed representatives to talk to God for them. They could do it themselves.

Right now, only Mike's squad can use the machine. But soon it will be available to everyone. Likewise, the Tabernacle no longer exclusively houses God. Now we find Him indwelling every believer. In fact, when we want to exercise spirituality, we can pray and He will talk to us. It is a great workout that works out just fine.

Holy Father, thank You for choosing to dwell in my heart and for giving me access to You. Thank you for splitting the veil. Dear God, I want to talk to You everyday and I want You to talk to me. And I want to enjoy Your presence every minute of this day. Amen.

TODAY'S READING: EXODUS 29:38-46; 38:24-31; 39:22-43; 40:1-38; NUMBERS 9:15-23; MATTHEW 27:51; HEBREWS 6:13–7:3; 10:19-25

Chatter

Guys only chattered at me when I was a rookie with the Bears. It didn't happen much after that. I earned respect early on. I was about respect. Even if someone was a bad player, I would show respect. I wouldn't talk down to anyone, unless they were going for my legs.

Some players talk all the time. Ray Lewis with the Ravens talks nonstop for the whole game. I don't know where he gets the energy but he backs up every word. Back in my day, Oakland's Lester Hayes talked all the time, but he was funny. He'd holler at Coach Ditka, "Hey! Mike! What you doin' out here? Come a long way to get a @#% whoopin'?" We were on the sideline cracking up.

Lawrence Taylor talked a lot. So did Otis Wilson. Otis would take every bit of your manhood if you'd let him: "I'm going to take your lunch money." "I'm gonna whoop you like a little boy." "I'm going to take you out."

Some players try to intimidate others with their chatter. They try to get into the other guy's head and get his mind off the game. They want to distract their opponent and get him to think about what is being said instead of the game. They use chatter as a tool to get an edge.

Guys could talk to me all they wanted. That was fine by me. I wouldn't allow anyone to get into my head that way. I wanted to play smarter than that. Even when I was "educating" a dirty player, I always did it within my realm of the play. I never chased people around and yapped at them unless I was angry, but that happened a few times. I actually loved it when someone started chattering at me. Some player's chatter was a sure sign that he was nervous about something.

Only a few guys are good enough to back up their talk. Ray Lewis is good enough. Lester, Lawrence and Otis were. I am not a chatterbox. I preferred to let my play do the talking for me.

If you claim to be religious but don't control your tongue, you are just fooling yourself, and your religion is worthless (Jas. 1:26).

One of the verses of an old children's song offers some good advice: "Be careful, little mouths, what you say." It is good to learn at a young age that words have consequences.

If we are honest with ourselves, we all can recall fiery situations that were fueled by what we said. We can all remember times when we wanted to take back our words. Of course, that is not possible. Usually all we can do is have regrets.

Most people know right away that they have messed up, but some people are oblivious until the consequences hit them. Shimei and his men chattered up a storm as King David left town. They took advantage of the situation when the king was in a weak moment. It's a good thing that David saw Shimei as God's correcting instrument or the chatterbox would have died sooner than he did. It's an interesting story.

David had sinned by committing adultery and murder. As a result, God's correcting hand had come upon him. His baby died, his family was publicly disgraced, his son led an uprising against him and, just to stay alive, David had to make a disgraceful retreat out of town.

It was during David's exit that Shimei and his men came on the scene. They shouted as the disgraced king, "Get out of here, you murderer, you scoundrel!"[1] One of David's men, Abishai, wanted to cut off Shimei's head, but David said no.

"Perhaps the Lord will see that I am being wronged and will bless me because of these curses,"[2] David said.

When David returned from exile, Shimei became scared and begged forgiveness for his chatter. Again David spared his life, but warned his son Solomon about Shimei's disloyal attitude and suggested some restraints be placed on Shimei. Shimei's chatter finally caught up with him. As it turned out, Shimei violated the boundaries and was eventually executed.

Chatter has consequences. Shimei discovered that—in spades. Does your mouth get you in trouble? Do you need to control your chatter?

Dear God, I want to glorify You with my mouth. Remind me to avoid idle and needless chatter. Guard me against saying hurtful words. Fill me with Your Spirit and help me control my tongue. Thank You.

TODAY'S READING: 2 SAMUEL 16:5-13; 19:16-23;
1 KINGS 2:8-9; 39-46; JAMES 1:26; 3:1-12

Rugged Cross

When I was with the Bears, a teammate expressed interest in God. That was good, but I momentarily forgot how God works. Instead of being a vessel through which God could act, I tried to actually be God in the eyes of the other player. I tried to clean up this player's life before he came to Christ, instead of letting God do the cleansing. God spoke to my spirit: "The next time I choose to use you to be a witness for Me, leave all that judgment and Pharisee stuff at home."

I changed my approach. I still want others to hunger for what I have in Christ, but I am not so overt. Rather than preach, I speak to others about God only after I earn the right by the way I live. I let my life reflect my faith.

That isn't always easy. At times I still want to be God in the eyes of others. Many of the young players I now coach have never known their father. Some have been abused—both physically and emotionally. No one else will ever know their pain. They won't tell. I have a huge responsibility to them, but I have learned to let God be God.

I do wear a wooden cross around my neck. It's not intended to show others that I'm a Christian; rather, it's there to remind me of whom I represent. It reminds me to be true to my word, to be fair, to be kind—to be as much like Jesus as I can be whether at home or at work.

I want to be a head coach some day. When I am, I won't wave a Bible at players or judge how they live, but I will demonstrate my faith by the way I live. If an owner doesn't want me representing the Lord, I'll have to tell him, "I'm not the one for your team."

My cross reminds me that my life on the inside is reflected in my choices on the outside.

Don't team up with those who are unbelievers. How can goodness be a partner with wickedness? How can light live with darkness? (2 Cor. 6:14).

There is a difference between wearing faith on our sleeve and wearing a reminder around our neck. Making our faith overt before we've earned the right is a shirt-sleeve response. Earning the right to minister and being there for someone at a God-ordained moment is what Mike exemplifies.

Wherever Mike goes, he wants to represent the Lord. He doesn't want to be hamstrung when it comes to his faith. If he were to work for an owner who wouldn't let him care for the needs of his players' hearts and souls, as well as their needs on the field, it would compromise who he is. In a way, it would make him what the Bible calls "unequally yoked."

The concept of being unequally yoked is *King James Bible* language for becoming united with someone who doesn't share our faith.[1] Other translations render it as "do not be bound,"[2] "don't become partners,"[3] and "don't team up."[4] In other words, God doesn't want us to be committed to potentially compromising relationships from which we cannot walk away.

We aren't supposed to walk away from our marriage, so marry a believer. Share the same Lord with your spouse-to-be or don't go into the relationship. There are too many potential big-decision conflicts in life to not share common Christian beliefs.

Values come out of faith, so we need to be on the same page as our business partners. Financial decisions and legal entanglements sometimes make it hard to leave a partnership, so we should make sure that our potential partners know the Lord before we become partners.

In the workplace, we shouldn't get locked in with stock options, perks or career goals to the degree that we cannot walk away if need be. If we can't represent God in the way He is leading, then we need to find another job. If we stay in a compromising situation, we are unequally yoked. God's solution is simple. We shouldn't become bound in the first place.

God gives us different crosses to wear. If we can't wear ours where we work, it just might be time to make a career change.

Stay free! Don't become unequally yoked.

Gracious God, give me the courage and determination to remain free from any yoke that might compromise my faith. Guard me from becoming bound to anyone who doesn't share my passion for You. Please remind me if my emotions begin to override Your Word. Thank you for Your protective hand and Your Son, Jesus Christ. Amen.

TODAY'S READING: EPHESIANS 5:3-15; 2 CORINTHIANS 6:14—7:1; 1 JOHN 1:5—2:6

I wasn't excited about leaving the Ravens. In Baltimore, there was a family-friendly environment, the team had a great defense, I loved my linebackers, and I had a solid relationship with the other coaches. Why did I leave all of this to go to a team that was 2 and 14? It seemed like a crazy move. But God had plans.

When my wife, Kim, and I realized that joining the staff of the San Francisco 49ers was an option, we began to pray. We prayed on our own. We prayed as a couple. We gathered the kids and prayed as a family. We were content to stay in Baltimore, but we were willing to go west if that was what God wanted us to do. We knew that what God wants is always what's best. We didn't want to miss God's plan. We wanted to be in His perfect will. As we prayed, we asked God to give us wisdom and to lead us. We didn't want emotion to guide us; rather, we wanted to hear His voice.

When Kim and I sat down with our kids, I said, "One of these days, when you're leading your own family, I want you to remember this time. I know some of you don't want to go. I know some of you aren't excited about uprooting again [we had moved from Chicago just two years earlier], but mom and I are concerned about God's best for us. We will not settle for what's good or for what's better than something else; we only want God's best."

The process of praying and deciding took a little less than a week. When a decision had been reached, we met again as a family. I made the announcement: "Mom and I have prayed and we are in agreement. We feel that God is calling us to San Francisco, so we need to move. We're certain that we'll find a great situation. Our family is going to be better for it. We don't know how it's all going to work out. We just know that if God is calling, that's all we need to know. God has plans for us."

Those who obey God's commandments live in fellowship with him, and he with them. And we know he lives in us because the Holy Spirit lives in us (1 John 3:24).

"But" is a very small word. Only three letters long, it can be a declaration of considerable consequence. It's usually an excuse for less than our best.

Coaches hate the word. My college coach sure did. When I messed up playing basketball and blamed my failure on anything but myself, I had to endure his wrath and run laps. "But, Coach" was nothing more than my attempt to make mediocrity acceptable.

Some excuses cost more than others. Some excuses cost souls. Jesus had invited a couple of guys to become His disciples, but both men had a few things they wanted to do before they followed Him.[1] Excuses are evidence of a problem with the heart. Neither man was sold out. Neither man was born again. "But I don't have time for Jesus right now" and "But I have things I have to take care of first" are excuses that won't cut it with God. Excuses for not embracing Jesus won't get us into the Kingdom.

Believers use the "B" word, too. When we offer excuses instead of repentance it doesn't cost us our souls, but it does cost in the Spirit. Whenever Christians make excuses for either something we shouldn't have done or for something we should have done, it grieves and quenches the power of the Spirit of God in our lives.[2] We are out of fellowship and powerless until we confess and make things right.[3]

Mike said, "But I don't want to leave Baltimore." However, he didn't stop there. He added what Jesus said to His Father, "Yet I want your will, not mine."[4] In Mike's case, not going to San Francisco wouldn't have cost his soul, but it would have cost the family God's best. For the Singletarys, God's will was far more important than their will. For that reason alone, they didn't make excuses. Instead, they prayed, obeyed and went.

"But, God" doesn't cut it. If you have an excuse for doing anything less than God's will, it will cost you either your soul or His blessing. Be like Mike and make God's plan more important than your plan.

Fabulous Father of Forgiveness, I confess those times when my will didn't match Your will. I'm sorry about the times I went my way instead of Your way. And I repent of making my thoughts more important than Your thoughts. Finally, forgive me for the times I've hesitated to do Your will. Thank You for forgiveness.

TODAY'S READING: LUKE 9:57-62; ROMANS 8:1-15; 1 JOHN 3:13-24

Osmosis

When I was young, I thought that being raised in a Christian home made me a Christian. I thought I got God by osmosis.

My mom wanted me to become a Christian when I was 13. I knew if I prayed it would make her very happy. So I prayed, but for the wrong reasons. I think I worshiped mom more than I did God. My prayer gave her comfort, but all it did for me was delay having a relationship with God.

As I grew older, I became more of a hypocrite. As a believer, I was lukewarm at best. I felt guilty all the time. I'd catch myself thinking, *It's OK. I'll totally commit one day. God, You know I'm interested. You know I really want to serve You, but not right now. I'm going to have fun.*

Despite my lukewarmness, I prayed a lot, but I always prayed for myself: "Lord, forgive me this time. I won't do it again." "Lord, just do this or that." "God, get me out of this." "Father, just fix this mess."

I participated in a Bible study, went to Fellowship of Christian Athletes meetings and attended church. Everyone thought that I was such a wonderful Christian. However, they only knew me in the light. I knew me in the dark.

I had the Christian chatter down pat: "Praise the Lord." "Hallelujah, brother." "God is good." I could talk faith, but there was no fruit, no joy and no relationship. I was faking it.

In 1986, after the Super Bowl, my wife and I were in Arizona for a conference. I couldn't sleep at night. I was restless. God was calling me. One day as I pulled into my driveway, I looked up and said, "Lord, I've had it. I'm done. This faking it is not going to make it. I'm tired of being lukewarm. Something drastic has to happen. I need You to show up. I need You, Lord. Whatever it takes, I'm willing to do it." That was the day I traded my osmosis for a relationship with God, and I've been serious about my faith ever since.

Not all people who sound religious are really godly. They may refer to me as "Lord," but they still won't enter the Kingdom of Heaven. The decisive issue is whether they obey my Father in heaven (Matt. 7:21).

There are three kinds of people:

- · those who coldly reject Jesus
- · those who are lukewarm, halfhearted about Jesus
- · those who are stoked, on fire, radical for Jesus

Let's take a pop quiz before we delve deeper into the question of eternity. I will take the quiz, too. Let's ask ourselves, to which of the three groups do we belong? Be honest. Cold, lukewarm or on fire?

Mike was honest with himself. He didn't like living in the state of osmosis, so he stoked the fires of his faith. At times I, too, have been lukewarm. It is not a pretty picture. I am glad I am now radical for Jesus. Where do you stand?

Now let's look at the question of eternity.

People who reject Christ have chosen their destination. Jesus made it clear: "No one can come to the Father except through me."[1] Paul confirmed what Jesus said: "The free gift of God is eternal life through Christ Jesus our Lord."[2] No doubts linger on this one: The cold ones don't go to heaven.[3]

Skip forward for a minute to the third group. Everybody who is radical about Jesus has also decided where he or she will spend forever. The apostle John gave us a checklist to help us know where we will go.[4] In summary, if we have committed ourselves to and are growing in relationship with God and Jesus; if God's Word is progressively becoming our standard for making life's decisions; if we are looking more and more like Jesus each day; and if we have a sense of conscience about our sin, have repented of our wrong acts and increasingly hate sin's presence; then we can know that we are saved from separation from God.[5] People who have received Christ fulfill the qualifications listed by John and will go to heaven.

What happens to the halfhearted? Nobody knows for sure, but it doesn't look good. Of the lukewarm, Jesus said, "I will spit you out of my mouth!"[6] There isn't much assurance in that phrase.

Are you willing to take a chance on osmosis or do you want to be stoked?

Merciful God of Salvation, I want Jesus Christ to be the priority in my life. I want to be on fire, stoked, fully committed to You. I'm grateful that I can know that I am Yours. Thank You for settling the issue of my soul.

Today's reading: Matthew 7:13-27; 2 Corinthians 13:5-6; James 2:14-26

BALANCE

BY MIKE SINGLETARY

I love coaching. I love it so much that I could spend all of my waking hours at it. This all-consuming nature of my sport means that most coaches' wives are basically widows. Too many end up divorced. My wife, Kim, would probably have left me if I had been a coach before now.

Why such a dismal track record when it comes to coaches and their family lives? Most of us fail to balance our lives. We let the season become more important than our families. Some never let up, not even during the off-season.

As a player, I spent hours watching film. I put in the time to make sure that I knew everything that was going to happen when I was on the field. If I had coached right away, I'm sure I would have done the same thing with every aspect of the game, not just defense. That degree of thoroughness would have consumed me and most likely would have cost me my family.

I see many failed marriages in the coaching ranks. It is a strange paradox. What good is it to win the Super Bowl, the national title or a state championship if your wife has left you and your children are strangers? Winning the trophy but losing the greater prize is too high a price to pay. It's not worth it.

As a player, I strove to make sure things were right at home, but I didn't work hard enough. Sometimes I messed up. Nonetheless, I was fortunate. I have a wife who does a great job. She held everything together when I lapsed and patiently waited for me to learn what I needed to learn to be a better husband and father.

My 10 years away from the game helped me balance my life. I discovered my kids' favorite ice cream flavors, got better acquainted with their hurts and fears and learned about their friends—we actually moved once to change their circle of friends. I became a better partner for Kim. We became a team at home. Kim no longer had to do everything on her own. I learned to be a better communicator and I discovered her deeper desires. To my surprise, what I had thought were her real needs weren't. With new insight, I changed my behavior and attempted to give her what she'd hoped for in a partner.

Finally, the time came to coach. I have already told you about this in a number of the readings in this book. I was fortunate to have started coaching with the Baltimore Ravens. I'll always be grateful to head coach Brian Billick for maintaining a family-friendly atmosphere. Mike Nolan also does this with the 49ers, as will I when I am a head coach. I'll want my staff to be good family men as well as good football men. That doesn't mean we won't work our tails off; we will, but we'll be better managers of our time. I'll want my coaches to keep a good balance between work and family.

As coaches, we preach balance to our players. What is true athletically is also true with the issues of life. Coaches, I challenge you to find a balance between your sport and your family, both in and out of season.

As coaches, we are dads, mentors and teachers to our charges. We have a great opportunity to not only teach our players the game but also to teach them about life. Having a healthy family life is the greatest testimony to the concept of teamwork. In that regard, showing our players what a happy home looks like is one of the most important lessons we can convey.

A healthy and happy home starts with mom and dad. The kids need to see mom and dad constantly relating, learning and growing together. If they are on good terms with each other most of the time, then the family is usually in pretty good shape.

When there is respect, without fear, things are usually pretty good. Kids will be kids, but they must respect their parents. I believe in a well-understood code or protocol. Boundaries need to be set and everyone needs to know what they are. Everyone must know what is acceptable and what is not. Respect in the house maintains boundaries.

Parents of healthy children intentionally set aside times to have fun and create memories. The family gets together and talks, plays hard and prays hard. Healthy families need to have a lot of fun. It is the fun times that make for good memories.

There are three areas of life that have helped add health to my family:

1. **Prayer**. There was a time when I thought that I could create a healthy home by organizing my time, arranging family events, planning vacations and setting up one-on-one time with my wife and kids. Some of these disciplines are good, but I had a tendency to put my family on a schedule—*my schedule*. My schedule still shapes much of what we do, but now I pray for wisdom as to how I can best serve my family and best take advantage of my available time. I pray to know what to do and for the courage to do it when it needs to be done. Moving to the leading of God's Spirit is proving to be more effective than any schedule ever could. Also, I make sure that we pray together as a family.

2. **Communication**. Kim and I sit down weekly to plan out the days. We both want to understand the schedule. We determine when we will go out on a date, who will pick up the kids, etc., and we resolve the occasional problem when Kim can't be in two places at once. Every day during the week, we stay in close communication, using our cell phones. Constant contact is crucial. It keeps me involved and keeps Kim from becoming resentful.

3. **Sacrifice.** As a husband, parent and coach, I must ask myself, *What am I going to give up?* I must be honest with my schedule and I must identify ways to best use my time. For example, coaches tend to waste time chatting and talking with friends on the phone between meetings and practices. I choose not to do that so I can finish my work and then leave to be with my family. I constantly ask myself, *Where can I cut back without hurting my coaching performance? How can I create more time with my family? How can I be more efficient to be more effective?* Shooting the breeze on the phone, lunch with the guys and hanging around for a few laughs can be fun, but it would steal me from my family. I have to ask, *What am I going to give up?*

Coaches, let me give you a word of advice: Be selective when picking your job. Unless you are a head coach, you will be working under someone else. Every coach has to work hard, but some head coaches are slave drivers and marriage killers. Identify them early on and be willing to walk away from a job on their staff rather than compromise your family life.

Coaches, don't lose touch with what's most important. Focus on the game, but don't forget your family. Don't end your coaching career with a mantle full of trophies and an empty living room. Regardless of how many wins you accumulate, a family lost to the game makes you a loser in the end. No matter how many wins you get on the field, make sure you are ultimately a winner at home.

Find the balance.

MIKE SINGLETARY

CAREER HIGHLIGHTS

MIKE'S BAYLOR DAYS

At Baylor University, Mike made 662 tackles. In 1978, he made an incredible 232 stops with 127 solo tackles. In 1979, he made 188 stops and in 1980 he was in on 145 tackles. In a game against Arkansas, he made 33 stops. Against Alabama, he made 30. Against Oho State, he made 31. He was the Southwestern Conference's Defensive Player of the Year for 3 straight years.

MIKE'S PROFESSIONAL CAREER

Mike Singletary was a second-round draft pick of the Chicago Bears in the 1981 NFL Draft and the thirty-eighth player selected overall. The only college junior to be selected to the All-SWC Team of the 1970s, Singletary earned All-America honors in both his junior and senior years at Baylor, where he averaged 15 tackles per game and established a team record with 232 tackles in 1978.

Singletary became a starter in the Bears lineup in the seventh game of his rookie season. In a game against the Kansas City Chiefs, his third as a starter, Singletary put on a remarkable defensive performance, recording 10 tackles and forcing a fumble. A nearly unanimous all-rookie selection, Singletary went on to start 172 games for the Bears during his 12-year career,

Mike was inducted into the Hall of Fame in 1998.

which is the second-most in club history.

An intense player, Mike finished as the Bears' first or second leading tackler each of his last 11 seasons. He amassed an impressive 1,488 career tackles, 885 of which were solo efforts. A constant force on defense, he missed playing just 2 games, both in 1986.

In a game against the Denver Broncos in 1990, Mike had a personal-best performance when he recorded 10 solo tackles and 10 assists. Selected to play in a team record 10 Pro Bowls, Singletary was All-Pro 8 times and All-NFC every year from 1983 until 1991.

The NFL Defensive Player of the Year in 1985 and 1988, Mike was the cornerstone of the Bears' innovative 46-defense. In 1985, he led a Bears' defense that allowed fewer than 11 points per game, as the team posted an impressive 15-1 record. He had 13 tackles and a sack in the playoffs leading up to the Bears' 46-10 defeat of the New England Patriots in Super Bowl XX. The Bears' league-leading defense held the Patriots to a record low 7 yards rushing, while the hard-charging Singletary contributed with 2 fumble recoveries.

Singletary was selected in the second round by the Chicago Bears in the 1981 NFL Draft. In his 12 years with the Chicago Bears, he was one of the all-time greats with a Hall of Fame career, starting 172 straight games and leading one of the greatest defenses of all-time in 1985.

(Source: National Football League Hall of Fame)

MIKE'S HONORS

All-Southwestern Conference Team, 1978, 1979, 1980
Davey O'Brien Award, 1979, 1980
All-American, 1979, 1980
Southwestern Conference Defensive Player of the Year, 1979, 1980
Southwestern Conference Defensive Player of the Decade, 1980s
Baylor All-Quarter Century Team, 1970-1995
Baylor Hall-of-Fame, 1991
Southwestern Conference Hall of Fame, 1996
College Football Hall of Fame, 1996
NFL Defensive Player of the Year, 1985, 1988
Super Bowl XX Champion, 1985
NFL Pro Bowl, 10 times
NFL All-Pro, 8 times
NFL Hall of Fame

ENDNOTES

DAY 1
1. See 1 Samuel 1:10-11.
2. *The Holy Bible, New Living Translation* (Wheaton, IL: Tyndale House, 1996), p. 290, footnote 1:20.
3. See 1 Samuel 7:3.

DAY 2
1. See Acts 8:1-3; Acts 9:1-2; Acts 26:9-11; Philippians 3:6; Galatians 1:13.
2. See Acts 7:58.
3. Acts 8:1.
4. See Acts 8:3.
5. See Acts 9:3-19.
6. Acts 9:20.

DAY 3
1. See 1 Kings 19:19-21.
2. Enoch is the other one.
3. See 2 Kings 2:8.
4. See 2 Kings 2:9.

DAY 4
1. See 1 Kings 18:40.
2. See 1 Kings 19:2-3.
3. See 1 Kings 1:15-16.

DAY 5
1. See Matthew 6:8.
2. See Ephesians 3:20.
3. See Matthew 7:7-8.

DAY 6
1. Luke 11:1.
2. See Matthew 6:7.
3. See Matthew 6:9.
4. Luke 11:8.

DAY 7

1. Various Chicago Bears' teams since the 1930s have been called the Monsters of the Midway. However, the nickname was first attached to the great 1920s' University of Chicago football teams coached by A. A. Stagg. "Midway" comes from the Midway Plaisance, which was the gateway to the 1893 World's Columbian Exposition in Chicago and is now the entrance to the University.

DAY 8

1. See 1 Samuel 2:18-26; 3:1-21.
2. See 1 Samuel 2:18.
3. See 1 Samuel 3:15.

DAY 9

1. See 2 Peter 1:3.

DAY 10

1. See John 8:44.
2. See Isaiah 14:13.
3. See 1 Peter 5:8-10.
4. See Job 1:7.
5. See Job 1:9-11.
6. See James 4:7.
7. See Ephesians 6:10-17.
8. See 1 John 4:4.

DAY 11

1. See Jeremiah 17:9.
2. See Isaiah 55:8.
3. See Proverbs 14:12.

DAY 12

1. See 1 Samuel 16:11, loosely translated.
2. 1 Samuel 17:28, *THE MESSAGE*.

DAY 13

1. See Luke 10:30-37.
2. Gerhard Kittel and Gerhard Friedrich, eds., *Theological Dictionary of the New Testament* (Grand Rapids, MI: Eerdmans, 1971), 7:548.
3. See Luke 10:37.

DAY 14
1. See Genesis 1:1. Both Moses and Joseph served in Pharaoh's "court."
2. See Psalm 94:3.
3. See John 13:7-9; loosely translated.

DAY 15
1. See Acts 9:1; 22:4; 26:10.

DAY 16
1. Matthew 5:43-44.
2. *The Bible Knowledge Commentary: New Testament,* John F. Walvoord and Roy B. Zuck, eds. (Wheaton, IL: Victor Books, 1983), n.p.
3. See 2 Peter 2:8-11; Jude 1:8-11.

DAY 17
1. 1 Kings 18:21.
2. 1 Kings 18:27.
3. 1 Kings 18:37.
4. 1 Kings 18:39.

DAY 18
1. See Joshua 7.
2. See Numbers 20:7-8.
3. Numbers 20:12.

DAY 19
1. See Judges 16:1.
2. See Judges 16:4-20.
3. See Matthew 11:11.

DAY 20
1. James 4:8.

DAY 21
1. 1 Samuel 17:4-7, *THE MESSAGE.*
2. See 1 Samuel 17:26.

DAY 22
1. *Encarta® World English Dictionary* (Developed for Microsoft by Bloomsbury

Publishing © 1999. Microsoft Office 2004. Microsoft Corporation. Redmond, WA), s.v. "glorious."
2. See Exodus 34:29-34.
3. See Exodus 16:20.
4. See Exodus 16:13-31.

DAY 23
1. See Joshua 6:1-21.
2. See Judges 7:19-23.
3. See Judges 4:12-22.
4. See Exodus 12:21-36.
5. See John 19:28-30.

DAY 24
1. See Jonah 1:3.
2. See Jonah 1:15-17.
3. See Jonah 3:1-2.
4. See Jonah 3:6-9.
5. See Jonah 3:10.

DAY 25
1. *NASB.*
2. Mark 3:17.
3. Adam Clarke, *Adam Clarke's Commentary on the Whole Bible,* n.p.
4. See Luke 9:54.
5. See Luke 9:55-56.

DAY 26
1. Theologians differ on the issue of predestination, election and free will. Since God is God, He can force choices on us when He wants to do so. But if He does, it's rare. Theologically, it is easier to understand why He doesn't than why He occasionally does. He doesn't want robots for followers. He wants us to choose Him.
2. "For all have sinned; all fall short of God's glorious standard" (Rom. 3:23); "For God made Christ, who never sinned, to be the offering for our sin, so that we could be made right with God through Christ" (2 Cor. 5:20-21).

DAY 27
1. See Romans 12:3-8.

DAY 30
1. H.W.O. Kinnard, "Surrender," Battle of the Bulge: Vets Remember, *PBS*. http://www.pbs.org/wgbh/amex/bulge/sfeature/sf_footage_04.html (accessed December 2, 2004).
2. "Who Were the Chosen 12?" *BibleNet*. http://www.biblenet.net/library/study/12disciples.html (accessed December 2, 2004).
3. "Legends about the apostle continued to develop long after his death. According to tradition, John lived to an old age in Ephesus, where he preached love and fought heresy, especially the teachings of Cerinthus." *Holman Bible Dictionary*, Trent C. Butler, ed. (Nashville, TN: Holman Bible Publishers, 1991), as found in Wordsearch 7 Basic Edition (Austin, TX, 1996-2004), s.v. "John."
4. See Isaiah 6:8.

DAY 31
1. See 1 Samuel 24:3.
2. See 1 Samuel 24:4.
3. I wish I had been a fly on the wall in that cave. If I had been, I bet that I would have heard David's men say something like this.
4. 1 Samuel 24:6

DAY 32
1. Colossians 3:23.

DAY 34
1. See 2 Corinthians 12:9 10.
2. 2 Corinthians 12:9.

DAY 35
1. See 1 Corinthians 4: 10.

DAY 36
1. See Esther 5:11.
2. See 2 Samuel 16:22.

DAY 37
1. Matthew 3:7.
2. See Matthew 11:11.
3. John 3:30.

DAY 38

1. See John 3:18-21.
2. Dr. Paul Lee Tan, *Encyclopedia of 15,000 Illustrations*, found in WordSearch 7 Basic Edition (Austin, TX, 1996-2004), #7023, "Nature and Light."
3. Ibid., #7026, "Speed of Light."
4. See Hebrews 13:8.
5. See Psalm 23:4.
6. See Psalm 119:105.

DAY 41

1. See Exodus 14:11-12; 16:3; 17:3; Acts 7:39.
2. See Acts 7:3.

DAY 42

1. See Romans 8:28.

DAY 43

1. Matthew 25:21.

DAY 44

1. See Luke 4:29-30.

DAY 45

1. James 1:2-3.
2. Acts 16:28.

DAY 46

1. Greek and Hebrew words for "joy," "rejoicing," "glad" and "joyful" in the *NASB* total 323.
2. *NASB*.
3. *Holman Bible Dictionary*, Trent C. Butler, ed. (Nashville, TN: Holman Bible Publishers, 1991), as found in Wordsearch 7 Basic Edition (Austin, TX, 1996-2004).
4. *Encarta® World English Dictionary* (Developed for Microsoft by Bloomsbury Publishing © 1999. Microsoft Office 2004. Microsoft Corporation. Redmond, WA).
5. See Titus 3:3; 1 Timothy 5:6; 2 Timothy 3:4.
6. See Ecclesiastes 2:1-11; Proverbs 14:13; Luke 8:14.
7. See John 16:20-22.
8. See Hebrews 12:2.
9. See Jeremiah 29:11.

10. See Luke 15:3-10.
11. See Micah 6:8.

Day 48
1. Luke 15:21.

Day 50
1. 1 Corinthians 4:17.
2. See Acts 16:1-2.
3. See Acts 17:14-15; 18:5; 19:22; 20:4; Romans 16:21; 1 Corinthians 16:10; 2 Corinthians 1:19; 1 Thessalonians 3:2,6; 1 Corinthians 4:17; Philippians 2:19.
4. See 2 Timothy 4:9.
5. See 1 Timothy 3:2-6.

Day 51
1. See Matthew 22:37-40.

Day 52
1. See 1 Samuel 5:1-12.
2. "Emerod: The older writers supposed by comparison of the account in 1 Samuel with Psalm 78:66 that they were hemorrhoids (or piles), and the older English term in the *King James Version* is a sixteenth-century form of that Greek word, which occurs in several medical treatises of the sixteenth and seventeenth centuries." *International Standard Bible Encyclopedia*, James Orr, M.A., D.D., ed., as found in WORDsearch 7 Basic Edition, (Austin, TX: 1996-2004), s.v. "Emerod."
3. See 1 Samuel 5:10-12.

Day 54
1. Hebrews 12:1.
2. *Holman Bible Dictionary*, Trent C. Butler, ed. (Nashville, TN: Holman Bible Publishers, 1991), as found in Wordsearch 7 Basic Edition (Austin, TX, 1996-2004), s.v. "discipline."

Day 55
1. Luke 9:20.
2. See James 2:19.
3. See Romans 3:19.

DAY 56

1. See Exodus 25–40.
2. See Exodus 39:22-43; 40:1-38.
3. See Exodus 38:24-31.
4. See Exodus 29:38.

DAY 57

1. 2 Samuel 16:7-8.
2. 2 Samuel 16:12.

DAY 58

1. See 2 Corinthians 6:14.
2. *NIV.*
3. *THE MESSAGE.*
4. *NLT.*

DAY 59

1. See Luke 9:59-61.
2. See Ephesians 4:30; 1 Thessalonians 5:19.
3. See 1 John 1:9.
4. Luke 22:42.

DAY 60

1. John 14:6.
2. Romans 6:23.
3. There may be a few exceptions to this rule but you won't be one of them because you have heard. For a better discussion on what happens to people who have never heard, see my book *Playing With Fire*, available at jaycarty.com.
4. See 1 John 5:13.
5. This is a summary of 1 John. Some scholars develop more points than I've included, but these are the main ones.
6. Revelation 3:16.

GLOSSARY

Football players and fans know the game's jargon. But many readers of this book will have never played a down or watched Monday night football. For the nonfootball-follower, we provide the following definitions as a football 101 guide to Mike's game-day stories. This list, of course, is not exhaustive. We have tried to glean and define terms used in the readings in this book. If there is something else that is not clear, get a football fan to help you—perhaps he will read this book as a devotional, too!

46 Defense. A defensive set using six lineman, four linebackers and one free safety. Buddy Ryan was the first to use it.

All-Pro. Think all-star—the best of the best. These are the players who are voted and selected by their peers, coaches and sportswriters to go to the Pro Bowl.

Blitz. When, in addition to the defensive linemen, one or more of the linebackers and/or safeties rush the quarterback during a play, attempting to sack him or rush his pass.

Bootleg pass. This occurs when the quarterback fakes a handoff to a back running around one end of the line while continuing to run toward the other end of the line. He now has the option to run or pass. If the linemen and the linebackers go for the fake, this usually leaves the corner back with the problem of covering the receiver or stopping the quarterback. If he covers, the quarterback runs. If he goes for the quarterback, the quarterback throws a pass.

Down field. Twenty yards or more from the line of scrimmage on the offensive end of the field is considered down field. The term is usually equated with routes receivers run and passes that are thrown, but it also is used in conjunction with down field blocking.

Downs. The team on offense has 4 attempts to gain 10 yards. Each of these plays is called a "down." Every time the offensive team gains 10 or more yards, it gets 4 more downs until it scores. If it fails to gain 10 yards, the other team gets the ball.

Draft. It is a time when the teams in the NFL select college players to be on their respective teams beginning the next season. The teams with the worst record select first in descending, consecutive order.

End zone. The end zone is a 20 yard rectangle at each end of the 100-yard field. When an offensive team advances the ball into the end zone, they get 6 points.

First down. A first down occurs when the offensive team gains 10 yards. The offensive team gets 4 more downs when they get a first down.

Free safety. The deepest defensive back who makes up the last line of defense. This player frequently roams the field and helps where needed. He usually lines up deeper than the cornerbacks.

Fumble. A fumble occurs when a player attempting to advance the ball drops it or gets it knocked out of his grasp before the referee calls the play dead.

Guard. See *Linemen*.

Hole, the. The offense tries to create holes in the defensive alignment for the running back to get through. Linebackers attempt to plug the hole before the running back can get through it.

Huddle. A huddle is when the offensive players on the field gather between plays to call the next play.

In the flat. The flat is the area of the field between the hash marks and the sideline within 20 yards of the line of scrimmage. When a receiver goes up and out, the pass will be thrown in the flat.

Interception. When a defensive player catches a pass thrown by an offensive player.

Keying. Both the offense and defense attempt to read and react to each other. A key might be the position of a player, a look of the eyes, a movement at the start of a play, or any number of giveaways. Reading the keys determines the reaction of the player doing the reading.

Kicker. There are two types of kicks and some teams have specialists for each. One is a punter who typically on fourth down will kick the ball back to the opposing team. The other is a field goal that is attempted by the place kicker. Kicking the ball between the goal posts is worth three points.

Line of scrimmage. An imaginary line running the width of the football field at the point where the football rests before a play begins. Crossing the line of scrimmage before the ball is snapped is considered off sides and results in a five-yard penalty.

Linebacker. The second row of defenders between the defensive linemen and the defensive backs is made up of linebackers. The middle linebacker is the quarterback for the defense.

Lineman. The players that line up on the line of scrimmage prior to each play are called linemen. An offensive line is made up of a center, two guards, two tackles and usually a tight end. A defensive line usually consists of two tackles and two ends.

Nickel defense. On a probable passing down, the defense pulls a linebacker and adds a fifth defensive back. This provides better pass coverage.

Play-action pass. When the quarterback fakes a handoff to a back running as a way to freeze the opposing linebackers for a moment. This allows the quarterback's receivers to get a head start on their passing routes and gives the quarterback more time to pass the ball before the opposing linebackers can attempt to stop him.

Playbook and game plan. The playbook is the team's collection of offensive and defensive schemes. The game plan is how the schemes will be utilized against a specific opponent.

Pro Bowl. The equivalent of the All-Star games in baseball and basketball. Only the All-Pro's (the best of the best) play in the annual game that is held in Hawaii.

Quarterback. The quarterback is the key player on the offense who begins each play by either handing the ball to a running back or by passing the ball to a receiver. The quarterback controls the offensive team.

Quarterback sneak. When the quarterback takes the snap, keeps the ball and plunges into the line behind or between his center and guards. This is often done on short yardage situations.

Read. A read is when a player recognizes what the other team is about to do. Typically, the quarterback will recognize a defensive set or see a blitz coming. Usually, he has time to alter a play as a way to counteract what he reads. On defense, usually it's the middle linebacker who reads the play the offense is about to run and counters it.

Running back. The running back lines up in the backfield behind the quarterback, takes handoffs from him and attempts to advance the ball by running with it. Sometimes he blocks for the quarterback and sometimes he receives passes.

Sack. When the quarterback is tackled before he can pass, lateral (underhand pass) or hand off the ball, he is sacked.

Snap. When the center (an offensive lineman) moves the ball from the ground at the line of scrimmage and puts it between his legs into the quarterback's hands or throws it between his legs in a spiral to the quarterback, a kicker or place kick holder, he snaps the ball.

Special teams. The players on the field during a kick off, punt and extra point attempt.

Strong safety. The strong safety is a defensive back who plays on the side of the field where the offensive tight end sets up. The offensive tight end determines the strong side of the field.

Tackle. A tackle occurs when the offensive player who has the ball is brought down. The term can also refer to a position (see *Lineman*).

Third-and-long. Third down with more than three yards to go to get a first down. This situation is usually considered a passing down. The defense will often set up a nickel defense when the offensive team is third and long.

Third-and-one. Third down with only one yard to go to get a first down. This is usually considered a running down. The defense will crowd the offensive line.

Turnover. When the defensive team takes the ball away from the offensive team either by recovering a fumble or by intercepting a pass.

ABOUT JAY CARTY

I knew I was a good speaker. For 27 years I spoke in churches, youth camps and other Christian venues—then I lost my voice. Frankly, I was always a little surprised that God didn't give me a greater profile. Standing 6-feet 8-inches, I was certainly one of the tallest people behind any pulpit, though many are larger in girth. But here I do not infer physical size; rather, I mean sphere of influence.

Among Christian speakers, there are eagles, falcons, hawks and buzzards. Billy Graham, Charles Colson and James Dobson are eagles. I was a buzzard. Nonetheless, sometimes I would catch myself thinking, *I'm a better communicator than so-and-so, but he's doing big gigs and I'm in little churches. What's going on, God?*

That's when I came to realize that my responsibility to God is a vertical relationship. His responsibility is horizontal influence. And God chose to limit and then stop my impact as a speaker, a vocation in which I suppose I was more reliant on my natural ability than I was on God.

When I could no longer speak before crowds, God thrust me out of my comfort zone and into a place where I am totally dependent on Him. He opened the door for the One-on-One series of books, even though I was not a trained writer. That was a huge step for a kid who grew up in the Mojave Desert of California.

GROWING UP

As a kid I didn't know Jesus as my Savior, but I began to trust God. I could pray "Now I lay me down to sleep," and I would call out to God to help me get through the night when my parents were fighting or were drunk again.

When I was in the third grade, a family from down the street convinced my mom and me to go to church one night. There was an invitation and my mom asked me if I would go forward. I thought she wanted to go, so I went with her. She went to get me saved. Neither of us was, but we each went for the other.

Because of my parents' drinking and fighting, we moved a lot. When I entered a new school at the start of the fourth grade, my teacher was worried about my development, thinking that being so much taller than everyone else would be bad for me. As a remedy, I was placed in front of the fifth grade class and was told to read three paragraphs from a book. I knew how to read, so the teacher was impressed and the next day I was in the fifth grade.

Early in junior high, my mom gave me a *King James Bible*. I enjoyed reading the Old Testament stories and looking up the naughty words. I always thought

I was getting away with something when I read the word "bastard." It actually appears twice.

I was in the seventh grade when my folks finally divorced. At this writing, I am 62 and it still hurts.

Dad was a bookie. That's a person who illegally takes bets on horse races. He also ran the poker games in the back of a bar. I was a bar kid and became an expert shuffleboard player on the old, long wooden tables with the round metal pucks that I learned to accurately lag with either hand. An old alcoholic named Bill and I never lost a game. He would get a beer and I would get a Coke.

I knew what my dad did was illegal, so one day after school I confronted him. I was the one who cleaned the bookie joint on Saturday, and I didn't want to be a part of an illegal activity. I told him that I wasn't proud of what he did and I asked him to stop and do the right thing instead. I approached him on Friday and he sold out on Monday, started a legitimate business and retired 10 years later with a car dealership. He even married the woman with whom he had been living. I was proud of my dad and was grateful to God.

When I was 14, I went forward during an altar call at an old-fashioned style revival meeting and received Jesus Christ as my Savior for real.

FROM BASKETBALL TO BOOKS

Jay and Mary Carty

I played and coached basketball at Oregon State University. I also assisted Coach John Wooden for three years at UCLA while I worked on my doctorate. And I played a year for the Los Angeles Lakers.

After my basketball playing days were over, I spent five years in business and eventually went into Christian ministry. I ran a Christian camp, was a church consultant and directed Yes! Ministries. In May 2002, I contracted a paralyzed vocal cord, ceased public speaking, stopped traveling and sought God for direction and healing. That is when an unexpected door opened: I cowrote the bestselling *Coach Wooden One-on-One* and *Darrell Waltrip One-on-One* while I waited upon God. And, I have now cowritten *Coach Wooden's Pyramid of Success*.

I am no longer anxious for healing. I'd rather stay home, write and hang out with my wife.

FOR MORE INFORMATION

JAY CARTY

1033 Newton Road
Santa Barbara, CA 93103

www.jaycarty.com
jay@jaycarty.com

Go One-on-One with Sports Legends

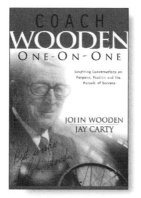
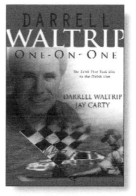
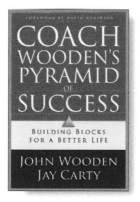
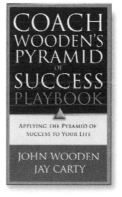

God's Word for Your World

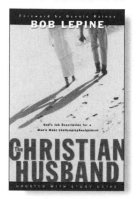

The Christian Husband
God's Job Description for a Man's
Most Challenging Assignment
Bob Lepine
ISBN 08307.36891

Anointed for Business
How Christians Can Use Their
Influence in the Marketplace
to Change the World
Ed Silvoso
ISBN 08307.28619

Living Life Boldly
No Regrets, No What-Ifs—
Selling Out to What Really Matters
Ted Roberts
ISBN 08307.31083

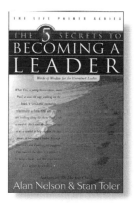

**The Five Secrets to
Becoming a Leader**
Words of Wisdom for
the Untrained Leader
Alan Nelson and *Stan Toler*
ISBN 08307.29151

**Moments Together
for Couples**
Daily Devotions for Drawing Near
to God and One Another
Dennis and Barbara Rainey
ISBN 08307.17544

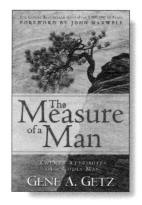

The Measure of a Man
Twenty Attributes of a Godly Man
Gene A. Getz
ISBN 08307.34953